CONTENTS

CONTENTS

It Happened In Series

It Happened In Ohio

Remarkable Events That Shaped History

Carol Cartaino
with contributions by Denvis O. Earls

Guilford, Connecticut

Copyright © 2010 by Morris Book Publishing, LLC

Project editor: Gregory Hyman
Layout: Sue Murray
Text design: Nancy Freeborn
Map: M. A. Dubé © Morris Book Publishing, LLC

Library of Congress Cataloging-in-Publication Data

Cartaino, Carol, 1944-
  It happened in Ohio : remarkable events that shaped history / Carol Cartaino.
     p. cm.
  Includes bibliographical references.
  ISBN 978-0-7627-4307-0
  1. Ohio—History. 2. Ohio—History, Local. I. Title.
  F491.C34 2010
  977.1—dc22

                                                            2010011495

Printed in the United States of America

10 9 8 7 6 5 4 3 2 1

For Dupy

ONTARIO

LAKE ERIE

ASHTABULA

LAKE   HARTSGROVE

GEAUGA

Put-in-Bay   Willowick

Toledo   Cleveland   CUYAHOGA

WILLIAMS   FULTON   LUCAS   OTTAWA

TRUMBULL

DEFIANCE   HENRY   WOOD   SANDUSKY   ERIE   LORAIN

Kent

PAULDING   SENECA   HURON   MEDINA   SUMMIT   PORTAGE

PUTNAM   HANCOCK   GREENWICH   MAHONING

VAN WERT   WYANDOT   CRAWFORD   ASHLAND   WAYNE   STARK   COLUMBIANA

ALLEN   RICHLAND

McGuffry   Lucas   CARROLL

HARDIN   MARION   HOLMES

AUGLAIZE   JEFFERSON

MERCER   LOGAN   UNION   MORROW   KNOX   TUSCARAWAS   HARRISON

SHELBY   DELAWARE   COSHOCTON   Gnadenhutten

Fort   Sidney   CHAMPAIGN

Recovery   MUSKINGUM   Barnesville

North   Licking   GUERNSEY

Star   MIAMI   Licking Summit   Norwich   BELMONT

DARKE   CLARK   Flint Ridge

COLUMBUS ✪

MADISON   FRANKLIN   FAIRFIELD   PERRY   NOBLE   MONROE

MONTGOMERY

PREBLE   Dayton   Xenia   GREENE   FAYETTE   PICKAWAY   MORGAN   WASHINGTON

Port   CLINTON   HOCKING   Amesville   Marietta

BUTLER   William

WARREN   ROSS   VINTON   ATHENS

HAMILTON   Hillsboro

Cincinnati   HIGHLAND   PIKE   MEIGS

CLERMONT   JACKSON

Serpent
Mound

BROWN   ADAMS

Ripley   SCIOTO   GALLIA

WEST VIRGINIA

LAWRENCE

KENTUCKY

Great Miami River

Scioto River

Muskingum River

Cuyahoga River

0   25   100 kilometers

0   25   100 miles

OHIO

ACKNOWLEDGMENTS

Carol Cartaino would like to thank editor Erin Turner for giving me a chance to really get to know my adopted state (as well as for the welcome touch of the West she brings to her competence, encouragement, and professionalism) and Denvis Earls for agreeing to help out with this journey down the years in Ohio. It enhanced my background for all of the subjects herein and made what was sometimes a very hard job more fun. Also much appreciated are the pleasantness and efficiency of project editor Gregory Hyman.

Thanks to Distinguished Professor Andrew R. L. Cayton of Miami University for graciously consenting to review the initial outline; Patty Krylach, one of my most promising writing students, for help with research, second opinions, and editing as needed; Dan Fleming, reference librarian, Licking County Library, for his very helpful and timely aid with Licking County subjects; and Clayton Collier-Cartaino for serving as a sounding board, researcher, and provider of the occasional bit of colorful copy.

The terrific collection of books on Ohio at the Highland County District Library included some truly charming old volumes. I much appreciated the able assistance of the entire staff there for all of their checking in and out (I think I have a blister on my library card), holding, renewing, and re-renewing of things. I'm also grateful to the SEO Consortium Interlibrary Loan system, whose excellence and helpfulness I never fully appreciated till now; my "silver Jeep"; and the west side of my office building for what they had to endure due to my immersion in this project.

Denvis Earls would like to thank Carolyn Perry Bartlett; Ponca Indian Elder, Middletown, Ohio, for her information on Native American legends; the Wilmington Public Library for books and source materials; Carol Cartaino, author and editor, Seaman, Ohio (godsend and friend); and Frank Henkel, author, Las Vegas, Nevada.

Also thanks to Patti Kinsinger, head of Academic Research, Watson Library, Wilmington College, for her help with the Wright Brothers, the Big Red Machine, and other subjects; James Palmer, student researcher, Wilmington College, for providing an outline of events for Kent State; Colleen Baker, student researcher, Wilmington College, for her help with the Gnadenhutten entry; and my wife, Linda, who served cheerfully as my proofreader and draft editor.

INTRODUCTION

I moved to southern Ohio in 1978 from what the people around here call "up East." I wondered before I left whether you could take a state with only four letters in its name seriously and knew only that Ohio seemed to be a fairly flat, bland place beyond the mountains of Pennsylvania.

More than thirty years later, I am still here. Though Ohio had little breathtaking scenery, and was not spectacular in any other obvious way, I soon discovered there were two very fine things about it: The people made you welcome, and the state wore well. It was a safe, pleasant, positive place to be—easy to take and easy to live in, day after day and year after year.

In the past months, working on this book, I've gotten to know my adopted state far better. And in the process have moved from appreciation . . . to admiration.

For a small state, Ohio has had a BIG impact on this country. There are a number of reasons for this, the first being its wealth of natural resources. When you read the descriptions of Ohio written by the first white people to see it—its broad, clear, fish-filled rivers; dense, hardwood-rich forests; lush green valleys; barely glimpsed mineral riches; and teeming wildlife of all kinds—you want to be teleported back to that time. Ohio's physical location has played a part too. It had a firm hold on the public imagination as the first American frontier—the first place beyond the original colonies everyone wanted to go to stake out new and better farmland and, later, as the gateway and stopping place en route to the greater west beyond. Between waterways, railroads, and other means, Ohio soon had a transportation system second to none, helping it become "the crossroads of the nation."

Not to be discounted in the equation are the vigor, earnestness, and imagination of its citizens. After its intrepid and highly able original inhabitants had been cleared out by the relentless drive of white western expansion, a stream of settlers followed from New England, the South, Pennsylvania and other states, and countries across the oceans. The names on the map of Ohio reflect these far-flung origins and their memories. Pioneers of all kinds came here in search of a new and better place, and in the decades and centuries that followed, they tried to make sure that Ohio was that place. Their sweat, ambition, and high-mindedness helped make Ohio first an agricultural power, then a political one, and finally an industrial giant, despite its small size. This was a place, too, where many improvements in society were first tested and then made the law of the land.

The descendants of all of those earlier Ohioans are now working together to find Ohio—half rural and half urban; half intellectual and half people who know how to work well with their hands—a new and even more exciting place in the world.

THE MYSTERY BENEATH
THE MYSTERY

250 million years ago

Somewhere between two hundred and three hundred million years ago, when no human had yet set foot on Ohio, a blast of incredible force rocked the south-central part of the state. Either a meteor or an asteroid from outer space struck the ground in northern Adams County or powerful forces deep within the earth's crust caused a tremendous blowup about a mile below the surface. Whatever the cause, the result was a crater four to five miles across, within which the rock layers, seven hundred cubic miles of rock—normally arranged in a nice, flat, orderly fashion—were scrambled helter-skelter. Rocks of different ages were all jumbled together, pushed up a thousand feet, pushed down five hundred, even turned upside down or on edge.

Had people been around to witness it, the concussion of this event would have felled trees, flattened dwellings, and knocked folks to the ground, even hundreds of miles away. This happening, scientifically labeled a "cryptoexplosion," has been called the most cataclysmic event ever to occur in the state.

Scientists today are still taking soundings and core samples and more in an attempt to finally resolve the cause of this epic disturbance. Thanks to the discovery of crystals normally found only at the site of nuclear bomb explosions and quartz cracked in a way that suggests stupendous pressures, the "meteor from outer space" theory currently has the lead. But this happening of the late Triassic period is still a mystery, and it has an even bigger mystery right on top of it.

At the western edge of the big crater, spread out on a hilltop overlooking scenic Brush Creek, is a sinuous giant earthen sculpture known as Great Serpent Mound. This is the largest effigy mound—a mound designed to depict something—in the country, perhaps the world, and is Ohio's most famous prehistoric landmark. Its photo has graced articles and books of all kinds, including encyclopedias and travel guides, for more than a century now and, as this is written, the site is being considered for the distinction of World Heritage Site. The Great Serpent's artfully looped and coiled body, twenty feet wide and two to six feet in height, is almost a quarter of a mile long. That it is a serpent and that it is an important historic treasure are about the only things most people seem to agree on.

First came the question of who built this. When the mound first came to the attention of white pioneers and explorers, they were sure that nothing so magnificent could have been created by Native Americans. Surely it must be the product of some lost branch of white civilization—Vikings, Phoenicians, wandering Israelites, or the like. Since the snake had an oval of some kind near its open mouth, it was even theorized that the Lord had made this as a big visual aid to dramatize the temptation of Eve and mark the Garden of Eden.

By 1846 a more scientific atmosphere prevailed. The site was surveyed and illustrated for a widely read book published by the Smithsonian, and Harvard archaeologist Frederick Ward Putnam studied it from 1883 to 1885. After some excavation of the serpent and three small conical mounds nearby, he pronounced it the work of the Adena culture, which lived in the area from 800 B.C. to A.D. 100, farming and creating earthworks of other kinds.

In the following years the mound would be attributed by others to the Hopewell culture, to an outpost of the prosperous and effigy-prone Mississippian civilization, and finally, via radio-carbon dating in the 1990s, to the Fort Ancient culture, which inhabited the area (and had a village below the mound) from A.D. 1000 to 1550. But even that is not definitive because, as some ethnologists point out, Native Americans sometimes reworked older sacred sites for their own ceremonial purposes. Therefore the mound could be older than the A.D. 1070 pinpointed by carbon dating.

Whoever built the mound, it is intriguing to imagine the scores or hundreds of people involved in carrying yellow clay, stones, and earth to an obscure location in the woodlands to shape this giant and graceful figure.

Frederick Putnam may not have been right as to the creators of the mound, but he did something far more important than making the world of science and history aware of it. He saved it from being lost forever to the settlers' plows. The area was covered with large trees when white men first saw it, but after those trees were swept away by a tornado, the farmer who owned the land was about to convert it to a sea of cornstalks.

Putnam took up a collection to preserve the site and, oddly enough, the citizens of Ohio owe one of their most notable pieces of physical history—Great Serpent Mound—to the unnamed women of late-nineteenth-century Boston who chipped in to buy the fifty-four acres on which the serpent lies.

So the serpent survived to be enjoyed by visitors and tourists and further speculated about. Might the serpent be a depiction of Halley's Comet, which appeared in a particularly flamboyant form in

1066, or even a sketch of the constellation Draco? One of the most fertile topics over the years has been the question of exactly what the head of the serpent is engaged in. Given the size of the head, it's been concluded that this must be a poisonous snake, since most nonpoisonous snakes in North America have heads not much wider than their bodies. Is it in the act of striking, swallowing an egg, trying to catch a frog, attempting to swallow the sun (seen as a Native American explanation of solar eclipses), or just the head of a horned snake, a figure in some Native American legends? The theories go on from there.

Even more puzzling is the question of this giant serpent's purpose. There were no human remains found in it, so it had no burial function, and no artifacts were found in or near it to hint at ceremonial purpose. Assiduous studies of the mound in recent decades by professional and amateur investigators have determined that the mound seems to have many astrological alignments. Parts of it are precisely aligned with the setting or rising sun of the solstices and equinoxes, and it also has meaningful lunar alignments. Some researchers have even claimed that one of the coils of the serpent reveals the first frost date for the surrounding area. The state's Native Americans today consider the serpent a key ceremonial center, and New Agers and other freethinkers also take the site very seriously. The New Age theories about the serpent alone could (and do) fill entire books.

The spiritual connection is easy to understand. When you visit the Serpent, located on winding Route 73 in quiet Adams County, the trip is more than just pleasant and scenic—full of farm fields, forests, and wildflower-filled meadows. As you stand on that ridgetop over Brush Creek, or on the slightly scary steel observation tower erected in 1903, you get the unmistakable sense that this is a center of some kind of spiritual power—that there is a mystery beneath the mystery.

A TRIP TO THE INDIAN ARSENAL

A.D. 800

Big Antler shifted his pack on his shoulders and checked to see if his two sons were still behind him. In a few hours they should be at the sacred quarry and all of this long and arduous travel would have been worth it. Before much longer the three of them were climbing up toward a long, twisting ridgeline amidst a line of rugged hills. The trails snaking here from all directions and the pits and piles everywhere in sight were evidence that this was the place. Big Antler had been here years before with other kinsmen, and he knew how to go about what needed to be done.

From their packs he removed several wedges made of bone and wood and the round, smooth hammerstones they had carefully picked from the river at home and carried all this way, heavy as they were. Then he looked up and down the ridge for a place to begin. On the side of one small hilltop he saw an exposed vein of what they had come for—the flint from which his people's weapons and most important tools were made. In other places, flint was buried far beneath the ground—here it was right in sight, for the taking.

Not that the taking was easy. The wedges had to be driven hard into any natural crack or fissure in the rock and then pounded hard with the hammerstones. Fortunately Big Antler and his sons, and the others who came here for this important harvest, were strong and able. They knew that the very top layer of flint was often weather damaged and shattered too easily, so they dug deeper. Before long they had pried loose a number of large chunks of flint and were ready for the next step—shaping. With mauls and smaller hammerstones they broke the big pieces one by one into blanks and cores just the right size and shape to be made, once they got home, into spear points, knives, arrowheads, and scrapers. They heated some of the chunks over hardwood fires to enhance their color and hardness.

As they relaxed around their campfire the night before they left the ridge with their precious cargo, one of Big Antler's sons raised the question, "Why did we not have to stand guard here? Would the enemies we watched for so carefully on our way here not know we were easy prey, with our heads down in these digging pits?"

It was a good night for stories, so Big Antler told him the reason. For many years the tribes had clashed over the right to mine this place until the Great Spirit, weary of all this bloodshed, had the Thunderbird tell the tribes that this place was for all, neutral ground. The bitterest of enemies could—and should—come and mine this indispensable resource side by side, in peace.

It is hard to realize now how much a simple stone of the right kind could mean in the days before iron and steel and all the other advantages of more recent technology. Until they were introduced to firearms and other modern inventions, the Indians of Ohio—and this entire country—made just about everything that called for a sharp edge or killing power from flint or obsidian. These materials were not just hard and capable of taking a high polish. When broken, they chipped in a way (the fancy term for this is "conchoidal") that yielded a half-circular, curved fracture. Put two of these together, edge to edge, and you had a tool of razor sharpness.

Dr. Louis Leakey of anthropological fame is supposed to have once demonstrated that an ancient stone tool of this kind could outdo a modern steel knife in skinning and cleaning a freshly killed antelope. In any case, for early Ohio Indians, a flint mine was indeed an arsenal. Without it, they could starve or be defenseless.

The arrowheads, spearheads, and other tools made by ancient Americans were not just formidable weapons; many of them are works of art in themselves. This is especially true of artifacts made of Flint Ridge flint. Unlike ordinary flint, which is usually gray or black, Flint Ridge flint comes in a jewellike spectrum of colors. It ranges from white with gray streaks to red, pink, blue, yellow, orange, green, and pieces with interminglings and bands of all the aforementioned colors. This is because the part of the shallow tropical sea that covered what is now Ohio during the Paleozoic era in the area where Flint Ridge is located was near the shoreline. The streams and rivers leading to it contained different sediments and debris, which were all incorporated into the mineral layers that would someday become the flint deposits.

Native Americans were quick to recognize superior toolmaking materials, as well as things of beauty. Flint Ridge flint was highly prized—and widely traded—turning up not only all over Ohio but also from the eastern seaboard to Louisiana and St. Louis. Flint Ridge was a key resource for Ohio Indians and other First Americans from about 10,000 B.C. until the introduction of flintlock rifles during the Revolutionary War gave Native Americans a new arsenal.

The ridge was most heavily exploited by the Native American Hopewell culture, from about A.D. 100 to A.D. 500. No one really knows who they were or all that much about them, but they created many magnificent artifacts (including items of Flint Ridge flint), many of which were funerary offerings. They also built extraordinary earthworks, without benefit of surveyors or bulldozers. Some archaeologists believe that the earthworks at Newark, Ohio—the greatest such achievement of this people—were created as a tribute to the flint riches of Flint Ridge, just nine miles away.

Flint Ridge flint was not overlooked by Ohio's white settlers, either. They used one of the lower grades of flint to make grindstones for flour mills and made flints for rifles and flint and steel fire-starting kits. And when the National Road came through Ohio, its builders used the plethora of flint chips in the area for their roadbed.

Even today, Flint Ridge flint—sometimes called Vanport flint, for the geological stratum it originated in—is sought after by jewelry makers and lapidaries worldwide. Ohio, which admittedly does not have a great number of exciting rocks, made flint the state gemstone in 1965.

In 1933 the state set aside 525 of the 2,000 or so acres of Flint Ridge that run roughly from Newark to Zanesville as a state memorial. Visitors here can see exhibits of ancient flint quarrying and the geology of the area, as well as the hundreds of Native American quarrying pits that still pepper the area, many of them turned into ponds by rainfall. One of the largest "knap-ins" in the country—gatherings of modern-day enthusiasts of humankind's first industry, flint-knapping—is held at Flint Ridge every Labor Day weekend.

THE BIRTH OF TECUMSEH

1768

The sky was clear above the Shawnee village this particular night in March 1768. There wasn't a cloud in sight, and the sun had long ago sunk below the horizon. The stars shone brightly, but one family was not asleep in its dwelling. No, this family was kept awake by the sounds of a new life being born into the world. The groans of a mother in labor filled the air, while the father—a distinguished chief—paced outside the birthing hut.

This was a difficult labor, but at last the birthing sounds were joined by the first cries of a newborn. Relief touched the faces of all present; a healthy boy had been born this night, and something felt special about the event. Indeed, as though even the heavens were taking note of the birth, a shooting star blazed across the sky.

Perhaps it was in memory of this brief celestial event, or simply a reference to his birth into the clan of the panther, but the young Native American boy was to be named Tecumseh, which can mean "shooting star" or "panther crouching for his prey." And although details such as what the true origin of his name was and where exactly in southwest-central Ohio he was born are lost to history, there can be little doubt that if there was some celestial sign at his birth, it was entirely appropriate. Young Tecumseh had an eventful life before him.

The boy's father, Puckshinwah, had fought in the French and Indian Wars of the 1760s, when the Shawnee were the greatest threat to the white settlers trickling into the Ohio Country. The colonial governor, Lord Dunmore, sent an army to the Ohio River in 1774 to quell the Shawnee uprising. The Shawnee were overmatched at the Battle of Point Pleasant, and many warriors died, including Puckshinwah.

Six-year-old Tecumseh was raised by his sister and Chief Blackfish. He was trained to be a warrior by his oldest brother, Chiksika. He soon became a marksman with weapons of all kinds and often led the war games of the boys of the village.

Before Tecumseh was fourteen years old, white raiders had destroyed his home five times. When George Rogers Clark attacked the town in 1782, the fighting was so intense that young Tecumseh fled in terror and hid in the woods. When he regained his composure, he vowed never to run again.

In his late teens, while playing a stick-and-ball game similar to lacrosse, Tecumseh was so fierce in his attack and intent upon winning that he didn't notice he had lost his loincloth. He continued to play until he had won. Such perseverance earned him the admiration of the other young warriors. But bold as he was, from the beginning he showed compassion for war prisoners and captives—this in a time when cruelties and atrocities were the norm.

In 1791, when he was twenty-eight years old, Tecumseh aided the Shawnee and Miami in defeating Gen. Arthur St. Clair's forces near St. Mary's, Ohio. This victory was the greatest ever by the Indians over the American military. Before long, Tecumseh became a war chief.

When "Mad" Anthony Wayne defeated the Miami-Shawnee Confederacy at the Battle of Fallen Timbers in 1794, Chief Little Turtle of the Miami, Shawnee War Chief Blue Jacket and others signed the Treaty of Green Ville, ceding the vast Indian country in Ohio to the federal government. The Indians gave up about two-thirds of the state—all except an area of the Black Swamp of northern Ohio and about ten square miles in northwest Ohio—to the Americans. Tecumseh refused to recognize the treaty and returned to his village near Xenia with many of his tribe.

By 1810 Tecumseh had become the paramount war chief of the Shawnee. He was angry with the civil chiefs who had signed the Treaty at Green Ville and ceded three million acres to the whites. Now Gen. William Henry Harrison was making "little treaties" with any Indian who would relinquish more territory. Tecumseh claimed the Treaties of Vincennes and Fort Wayne had been signed by fearful old men, not the true leaders of the tribes. He believed that the land belonged to all Indians, and unless all the Indians signed over their rights, no one chief or tribe could sell any of the land. He told the chiefs that he would kill any man who signed away Indian land.

"Nobody speaks for all of the Shawnee," he said. "Nobody speaks for all Indians. The land is the gift of the Master of Life. Didn't the Great Spirit make the land for all of his children? Can you sell the air? Can you sell the water? Nobody can sell the land." Tecumseh believed that the Indians west of the Appalachian Mountains must unite in a Pan-Indian army, forget their ancient differences, and fight the white man.

One of Tecumseh's brothers, Tenskwatawa, who later became known as "the Prophet," had a vision from the Master of Life that if the Indians united into one nation, they could drive the Americans back across the Appalachians. The Prophet said they should leave the Ohio Country, give up the ways of the white man, give up liquor and firearms, and return to the old ways. If the Shawnee did these things, the Prophet said that the Great Spirit would protect them and the white man's bullets could not hurt them. Tecumseh and the Prophet moved their village into northern Indiana. Many of the northern tribes joined Tecumseh and the Prophet at their village, Prophetstown, on Tippecanoe Creek.

Tecumseh visited many of the tribes from Canada to the Gulf of Mexico and up and down the Appalachians seeking allies. Whether presenting to his own people or to the "Long Knives," as the Indians called the Americans, Tecumseh was unsurpassed as a speaker—intelligent, dramatic, forceful, and proud. In March 1811, as Tecumseh began a trip to the south, a shooting star crossed the southern skies as if announcing his coming.

Many of the southern tribes had taken to farming in the European manner, living in houses, and keeping domestic animals. Their elders had signed treaties with the white governments and wanted to live in the same manner as the whites. While they were impressed with Tecumseh's ideas, few were in the mood to join his war. While Tecumseh was among the tribes of the South, Territorial Governor William Henry Harrison, who had become alarmed at the size of the Indian alliance with which Tecumseh had surrounded himself, made his move. He took an army of one thousand men to a camp just outside Prophetstown, intending to disperse the Indians. In the hours before dawn on November 7, 1811, the Prophet led his soldiers in a surprise attack on Harrison's camp. Harrison's army withstood the siege and defeated the Prophet, who then lost all credibility with the other Indians.

In December 1811, before Tecumseh could learn of the defeat of his army, a massive earthquake along the New Madrid Fault shook the South and Midwest. The Redstick Creeks took this as a sign that they should join the great Tecumseh in his war against the whites.

Finding Prophetstown reduced to ashes upon his return, Tecumseh vowed to go to Canada and ally with the British.

Tecumseh rallied his Indian allies to join the British forces in the siege of Detroit. Tecumseh and four hundred of his warriors continuously feigned attacks on the fort until Gen. William Hull, governor of the Michigan Territory, became terrified that his command would be annihilated. He surrendered the fort without a fight and ultimately was court-martialed for the most humiliating surrender of the War of 1812. It was a great strategic victory for Tecumseh. After capturing Detroit, Tecumseh captured Fort Malden. Tecumseh's Indian army proved to be brave and tenacious, even though the English often retreated rather than meet the enemy head-on in battle.

As General Harrison marched his armies north, Tecumseh and the British crossed the Detroit River and took shelter in Canada. When the British tried to retreat deeper into Ontario, Commodore Oliver Hazard Perry's naval forces on Lake Erie cut off their supplies and their escape route.

Forced to make a stand, Tecumseh and his British allies met the Americans in the Battle of the Thames near Chatham, Ontario, on October 5, 1813. General Harrison, "Old Tippecanoe," surrounded the Indians who were covering British General Proctor's retreat and inflicted a devastating loss on Tecumseh's forces.

Col. Richard M. Johnson (among others) claimed to have personally killed Tecumseh on the battlefield. Johnson's fame would carry him to the vice presidency under Martin Van Buren. Johnson reported that Tecumseh's body was cut to pieces on the battlefield. But the Shawnee say they carried the body of Tecumseh from the field and buried him on sacred ground in Ohio, where someday he will rise and lead the Indians to victory over the white man.

Tecumseh envisioned a confederation of Indian nations that could rival and defeat the Americans. He did not succeed, though this bold idea might have been the last real chance the Native Americans had to win the war against the white settlers.

Tecumseh has since been not only embraced but romanticized by both his admirers and his former foes—he is the "noble savage," the "model Native American."

MASSACRE AT GNADENHUTTEN

1782

When Thomas and Abel came straggling into Schoenbrunn, they were just barely alive and it was hard to tell whether they were human. Their clothes were torn and tattered, their hands and feet were muddy and cut, and dried blood drenched their faces, heads, and clothes. The two Moravian Indian boys, nine or ten years old, had both been scalped. Thomas could scarcely walk, but he was helping Abel limp along. The exhausted boys panted and cried as they described the horrifying scene from which they had escaped. The Americans had killed everyone they knew.

On the second day of March 1782, Col. David Williamson and a corps of one hundred militiamen arrived at Gnadenhutten, Ohio, where they found the men of this peaceful settlement of "civilized" Indians in the fields planting their crops. They camped on the outskirts of the village. The next morning, Colonel Williamson's party rounded up the Moravians, disarmed them, and tied them together in pairs. The main buildings became jails.

While searching the village, Williamson's men found bloody women's clothing and branded horses. The Indians produced the branding irons, but the militia believed the items to have been taken in murderous raids. Colonel Williamson noted in his log that he believed the Indians' protestations of innocence, but his men's blood was up. As was the militia tradition, the men voted on the disposition of their captives. The lopsided vote (82–18) was to dispose of the Moravian menace. The Indians were informed that they were to die and were permitted to hold their evening devotions.

On the morning of March 8, 1782, the eighteen soldiers who asked for mercy for the Moravians washed their hands in the manner of Pontius Pilate and withdrew a distance before the slaughter began. Using a cooper's mallet and a blacksmith's hammer, militiamen went down the rows of trussed-up men and smashed their heads. They then crossed the town square to the building where the women and children were being held. One by one they crushed the heads of the women and children. Then the scalping began. Every man, woman, and child was scalped. Some who had been scalped were still alive and were "mercifully" dispatched with another blow of the mallet. Colonel Williamson then ordered that the buildings be set afire and the bodies burned where they lay.

Only two young boys had been able to crawl under the building before the fire was set. As the blaze consumed the building, Abel made it out of the crawlspace and into the woods. The other boy got stuck trying to get out, and was caught by the militiamen, who chopped off his head. Another boy, Thomas, who had been inside one of the buildings during the massacre, silently crawled over the dead bodies and stumbled into the woods, where he and Abel waited until nightfall before making their way through the forest to Schoenbrunn to warn the other Moravians.

The Moravian Indians were Christians. In the mid-1700s, Moravian missionaries (Czech Hutterites) successfully converted a few Mingo,

Delaware, Munsee, and Mohican Indians to Christianity. The "Moravian" Indians built "praying towns" in east-central Ohio.

Missionaries founded Schoenbrunn, the city of the "beautiful springs," in 1772 as a Moravian Indian town. By 1778 it held more than four hundred converts and sixty buildings, including the first Christian church and school built in the Ohio Country. The homes in this village had glass windows and housed musical instruments and books, and the town artisans produced quality silverwork and other crafts.

When they converted to Christianity, these Moravians gave up their native languages and religions. Their children learned English. The Indians adopted the Christian practice of monogamy, abandoning their tradition of multiple wives. The men learned European-style farming and fenced their land, while their wives tended to the children and to matters around the house. By all appearances, the Christian Delaware, Mingo, and Mohicans were just like their white farmer neighbors.

The Moravians called themselves the Church of the Brethren in Christ, or "Brethren." One of the first Indian converts was Netawatwees, a visionary leader and powerful warrior. He was often in conflict with Buckongahelas, war chief of the Delaware, who kept the main body of the tribe encamped along the Sandusky River. Buckongahelas was a constant ally of the British and despised the Moravians for their pacifism. The Brethren did not believe in war as a means of settling disputes and refused to fight.

The nearby town of Gnadenhutten ("Huts or Tents of Grace") was founded in 1772. The Indians maintained gardens of corn, squash, and beans and kept cattle, workhorses, chickens, and pigs. Evenings were spent in devotions and prayer.

Lichtenau (German for "fields of light") was established in 1779. The Moravian Protestant congregations continued to grow.

When the British and Americans fought in the Revolution, both sides tried to get the Moravians to join them, but the theology of the Brethren was for peace, not the violence of war. Any wounded from the area battles, including hostile Indian tribes, were treated with kindness and generosity.

Buckongahelas, war chief of the Delaware, warned the Moravians that he intended to carry the British Union Jack into western Pennsylvania and across the Ohio River into Kentucky. In return, the British offered protection and promised to leave the Ohio Country to the Indians after the defeat of the colonists.

Netawatwees had died in 1776. The Moravian Indians sought protection from his grandson, Killbuck; but Killbuck failed to provide enough food or shelter for the growing number of Christian refugees. The Moravians had no alternative but to return to Schoenbrunn and Gnadenhutten. They reoccupied their villages and resumed their way of life. For the next two years, as the war raged around them, the Moravians gave sanctuary to injured colonist and redcoat alike. Unfortunately, their Christian generosity caused both sides to be suspicious of the Moravians.

In the fall of 1781, the British sent their Mohawk and Tuscarawas allies against frontier settlements. That winter, the Mohawks attacked isolated settlements, killing the men and taking the women and children prisoner. Any child that fell behind on their march to the British camp was clubbed to death.

The raiding Indians sought shelter at Gnadenhutten, bringing with them captives and scalps. The Moravians took them in, but as spring approached they demanded that the marauders leave. The Moravians gave the murderers supplies for their journey in exchange for some articles of clothing.

A punitive expedition was soon mounted by the militia. Colonel Daniel Brodhead led the militia from Fort Pitt into the Coshocton

Valley and destroyed the Delaware Indian town of Coshocton and the Moravian town of Lichtenau without regard to the inhabitants' cries of innocence. Colonel Williamson and his militia were dispatched to punish Gnadenhutten. Before these militiamen returned to their homes along the Ohio and Monongahela Rivers, they had destroyed three towns and left no living soul within a twenty-five-mile radius of Gnadenhutten.

The slaughter of ninety neutral, peaceful Moravian men, women, and children at Gnadenhutten infuriated the other tribes of the area. The Wyandot, Delaware, and Shawnee joined the British in retaliatory raids. Bloody border battles continued along the Ohio River and the Allegheny Mountains for the rest of the Revolutionary War.

The massacre at Gnadenhutten has rightly been called "one of the blackest incidents in American history." The city of Gnadenhutten has preserved the site as a sacred place. It contains the mass grave of the slain and a handsome bronze plaque marking a well-tended burial mound. The cemetery also became the final resting place of many Revolutionary War veterans, who now lie alongside the Moravians they murdered. The inscription of the marker near the burial mound reads, "Here triumphed in death ninety Christian Indians, March 8, 1782."

The town of Schoenbrunn has been completely rebuilt and is maintained by the Ohio Historical Society. It is open as an educational center for scholars and tourists. Lichtenau was never rebuilt.

A ROYAL CHRISTENING

1788

Why would a town in a new nation name itself for the queen of a foreign country after that nation had just fought a Revolution to throw off their own monarchy? Well, it happened in Ohio.

George Washington and his brothers were land surveyors in the early 1770s. George had explored and mapped the far reaches of the Virginia frontier, into the Ohio River Valley. There he saw some of the most beautiful and verdant land in the country. He thought it was a fertile site for future settlement and mentioned its glories to his friend, Gen. Rufus Putnam. After the Revolutionary War, Putnam and ten other men met at the Bunch of Grapes Tavern in Boston to form the Ohio Company of Associates. They intended to raise enough money to buy land as soon as it was available in the new territories west of the Allegheny Mountains.

When the Continental Congress established the Northwest Territory in 1787, Putnam and friends were ready. They purchased 1,781,760 acres of what would someday be southeast Ohio for $1 million. Then, in order to attract settlers, they sold the land for less than Congress was selling other land in the territory.

The settlers were not long in coming. After struggling over the mountains and across Pennsylvania with horses and oxen dragging heavy carts, a party of carefully chosen settlers reached the Ohio River, the "highway" into the new lands. Forty-seven men then journeyed downriver in flatboats to where the Muskingum River and Duck Creek met the Ohio. There, across from Fort Harmar—a pre-Revolutionary fort built to protect the river from the Wyandot and Delaware Indians and the British—they settled in to build Adelphia (named for one of the barges on which they had descended the Ohio). They soon renamed the town Marietta in honor of Marie Antoinette, the young and beautiful queen of France.

France had come to the aid of the American colonies, both financially and by providing war materiel, during the War for Independence. In 1781 Louis XVI sent his fleet of naval gunboats to bottle up the English fleet on the James River in Virginia and helped General Washington defeat the British at Yorktown. So it seemed natural and gracious of the new United States to name one of its most promising new settlements in honor of the French queen.

Marietta became the first permanent American settlement in the Ohio Country. The Indians were not so pleased to see this new settlement. To protect the settlers, the government immediately built two new forts nearby—Picketed Point and Campus Martius (Latin for "field of Mars," the Roman god of war).

In 1788 President Washington said, "No colony in America was ever settled under such favorable auspices as that which has just commenced at the Muskingum." Settlers arrived regularly, and by late 1788 the population had grown to 137 people. By 1795 the issues with the Indians were mostly resolved, and the city continued to grow.

According to local legend, Marie Antoinette acknowledged the honor bestowed on her by the city fathers by giving the city a magnificent bronze bell. The town constructed a bell tower in the corner blockhouse of the Campus Martius palisades to house it. When the ship carrying the precious bell sank en route to America, the queen ordered a new bell from a Boston foundry. The replacement bell was delivered and celebrated as the queen's gift. Many locals believe that the bell still on display today at the Campus Martius Historical Site is the queen's gift.

Some historians question the validity of this legend. According to Glen Wolf, a researcher at the Washington County Historical Society, the bell at Campus Martius was ordered by Mrs. Rufus Putnam, wife of one of the Ohio Company investors.

Whatever the source of the bell, it rang out loudly in November 1793. Though the sad news took three weeks to reach this bustling river town, it did arrive. The townspeople learned that on October 16, 1793, Queen Marie Antoinette had been beheaded, a victim of the French Revolution's "Reign of Terror."

To express their grief, the citizens of Marietta began to ring the great bell at Camp Martius. It was not the joyous ring of revolutionary liberation but a sad tolling of the death knell for a former ally and cherished friend more than four thousand miles away.

In 1800 the Ohio Company opened a land office in Marietta to facilitate sales of plots. When the Harrison Act made land available on credit, sales boomed. Marietta became a fast-growing and prosperous city.

When Marietta gained its charter as the first city in the territory, its freeholders voted to establish a republican form of government, which gave the vote to every man who paid taxes and owned property. The town levied a tax to support schools and provided for election of its own officials rather than accept those appointed by the territorial governor. Marietta also provided for its own law enforcement to maintain order and keep the peace. A circuit court soon followed. Marietta was briefly the territory's unofficial first capital when Governor Arthur St. Clair set up his offices there.

Religion and education were important to the people of Marietta, and the Ordinance of the Northwest Territory provided for the support of both. The Congregationalists were the first denomination to build a church in Marietta, soon followed by the Moravians, Mennonites, and other sects. In 1797 the Muskingum Academy was established; it grew to become Marietta College (1835). The ordinance also provided for the protection of some Indian historical artifacts in the new territory. Today the Great Mound, or Conus—a conical Indian burial mound—is the central structure in Marietta's cemetery.

Soon factories and mills rose on the banks of the Muskingum and Ohio Rivers. Harman Blennerhassett was building barges and seaworthy ships at his docks in Marietta by the early 1800s. Blennerhassett conspired with Aaron Burr to separate the lands west of the Allegheny Mountains from the new United States. He built a fleet of vessels to use in that effort in 1806, but Ohio's leaders caught on to what they were doing and, with the assistance of the Virginia Militia, arrested Burr and Blennerhassett before they could bring their plan to fruition. Burr was tried and acquitted, but Blennerhassett lost his business and reputation.

In 1808–09 the state of Ohio chartered its first banks and opened a bank in Marietta. Having capital available for investment gave rise to an even more vigorous shipbuilding business. Vessels of fifty tons became common on the Ohio River, and soon three-hundred-ton ships were being built to carry cargoes of hides, cotton, and barrel staves down the Ohio to the Mississippi, then through the Gulf of Mexico, up the East Coast, and on to Europe.

In 1860 oil was discovered in Marietta, resulting in a whole new class of wealthy citizens. The Dawes brothers founded Pure

Oil Co. and rose to both business and political prominence. Expensive mansions soon dotted the Allegheny Plateau and the rolling hills around Marietta.

Sawmills and brick makers aided the growth of the city. Today more than seven miles of brick streets still pave this picturesque riverside settlement, and Georgian-style brick homes still dominate the central city.

The history of Marietta and the surrounding area is preserved in a museum setting at Campus Martius and the Ohio River Museum, open year-round. The storied bell is on display, as is a full historical panorama of the colorful events and accomplishments of the first settlement in Ohio. The Ohio River Sternwheel Festival in September celebrates Marietta's link to inland shipbuilding.

ST. CLAIR'S SHAME

1791

The Battle on the Wabash River at what is now Fort Recovery, Ohio, was the worst defeat every suffered by the U.S. Army at the hands of the Indians. Of Gen. Arthur St. Clair's original army of three thousand men, only forty-eight survived—a casualty rate greater than 97 percent. Fully one-quarter of the entire U.S. Army was destroyed in a single battle—the best of the veterans of the American Revolution annihilated by warriors with antiquated weapons. This devastating loss came to be called St. Clair's Shame.

After the Continental Congress established the Northwest Territory in 1787, settlers flooded into the Ohio Country. They pushed up the ample rivers of Ohio, destroying Indian settlements as they advanced. The Miami and Shawnee had lived along the Great Miami and Little Miami Rivers for centuries. They were farmers, depending primarily on huge, well-tended gardens and the abundant game that inhabited the forests around them for their food. White settlers coveted these lands.

Every spring settlers from Kentucky and Virginia raided along the rivers, burning the Shawnee and Miami settlements. Each summer the Indians resettled their ancestral lands. But after the invasion of the Virginia Militia and the defeat of the Shawnee at the Battle of Point Pleasant, the elders of the Shawnee and Miami recognized the strength of the Americans and moved their villages farther up the Great and Little Miami Rivers.

Congress tried to keep the settlers along the Ohio River. Troops were sent to keep squatters out of the interior, but it proved to be impossible. No sooner had the army driven settlers out than they were back, rebuilding. The Shawnee fought back, but their defense of their homes was labeled "massacres" by the Eastern press. Col. John Hardin was dispatched with four hundred men to chastise the Indians. On October 22, 1790, Hardin's corps was ambushed by 1,100 warriors led by Chief Little Turtle of the Miami. Hardin lost 129 men in minutes; another 150 died during the all-out retreat back across the Ohio River.

Little Turtle was the son of Turtle, the great war chief of the Miami, who had driven the Iroquois out of northern Ohio. Most of the Ohio tribes had both a civil chief and a military chief. Le Gris was civil chief of the Miami. He had divided the Miami into four clans, each with its own village and its own civil authority.

After Little Turtle was born in 1747, Turtle taught him military strategy and the art of war. Little Turtle stood over six feet tall and was a spellbinding orator. His bravery and cunning in battle gave him status among his people. He gained recognition in civil councils as well as in the tribe's war councils.

As the white settlers advanced into Ohio, Chief Le Gris and other elders of the Miami counseled compromise, giving up land, and moving farther west to avoid battle with the Americans. Little

Turtle was furious. He had proved that when the Indians combined their strength they could defeat the encroaching whites. He had led just such a coalition of tribes against the French during the Seven Years' War. Little Turtle argued that the Shawnee and other Ohio tribes were as sick of the invaders as he was and that they were sure to join forces with him to defeat the Americans.

In the 1780s Little Turtle and War Chief Blue Jacket of the Shawnee established the Miami Confederation. By the middle of the decade, Buckongahelas, chief of the Lenape (Delaware), had led them and the Wyandot into the confederation. The Miami Confederation became a truly Pan-Indian movement when the Kickapoo, Chippewa, and Potawatomi joined them from the West. A few Cherokee and Creeks from the South also joined the confederation.

After the embarrassment of Hardin's defeat, President Washington ordered the governor of the Northwest Territory, Gen. Arthur St. Clair, to mount an expedition to subdue the Indians in the Ohio Country.

Arthur St. Clair Jr. had been a trusted aide of Washington during the Revolution. He had an excellent military record but was known to be an arrogant snob who preferred the comforts of the East to the duties of governing a territory. St. Clair chose Maj. Gen. Richard Butler as his second in command. Butler was a formidable warrior, respected and feared by the Indians. He had proven in many battles to be brutal, relentless, and merciless.

St. Clair and his three thousand men chased the Miami and Shawnee around the territory most of the late summer and fall. Little Turtle outwitted St. Clair as he fought a war of attrition. St. Clair lumbered along with his poorly disciplined army and its camp followers, cooks, laundresses, newspapermen, and prostitutes. He marched for a couple days, stopped and built a fort for resupply purposes, and then, after a rest, advanced again. The Shawnee and

Miami scouts reported his every move to Little Turtle. During his ascent of the river, St. Clair was attacked all along the way, losing men in every battle. His troops were so disheartened that desertions began to whittle down their numbers. Most of the men had enlisted only for six months, so by the time of the ultimate conflict, St. Clair's army was down to 1,453 men. In addition to their poor training and dwindling numbers, his forces suffered from shoddy equipment and inferior provisions, thanks to profiteering suppliers.

On November 1, 1791, St. Clair moved his army to St. Mary's. The Miami Confederation encampment was a few miles away. With the enemy at what he thought was a safe distance, St. Clair didn't bother to build defensive positions. He intended to rest his troops for a couple of days, then attack. On the morning of November 4, the soldiers rose for breakfast and stacked their weapons, as was the order of the day.

As soon as the men sat down with their meals, Little Turtle attacked. The militiamen broke and ran, leaving their rifles in their stacks. When the Army Regulars formed, Little Turtle's force flanked them and attacked from the rear, reducing their numbers in short order. Before the artillery could be brought to bear, Shawnee marksmen led by Black Hoof decimated the gun crew and destroyed the cannons.

St. Clair had two horses shot out from under him. His remaining men charged the Indians with fixed bayonets, but after several charges they were driven back and collapsed in disarray. Facing total annihilation, St. Clair ordered a retreat, leaving Butler's meager regiment to face the brunt of the attack. Butler was struck down by a Shawnee ax—his chest split open and his heart removed while it was still beating. The Indians divided his heart among them and ate it, believing that by eating a brave enemy's heart, they would gain his strengths. Only twenty-four soldiers and two dozen civilians of St. Clair's entourage escaped. In the haste of their retreat, they abandoned food, weapons, and equipment that would have supplied 1,500 men for six months. Eight hundred thirty-two soldiers and two hundred camp followers were killed. Only twenty-one Indians lost their lives.

The site of St. Clair's Shame is marked by a marble monolith at Fort Recovery. A bronze marker was placed on Main Street at the very spot where General Butler was struck down.

THE BATTLE OF FALLEN TIMBERS

1794

After the devastating defeat known as St. Clair's Shame, it wasn't just St. Clair who felt the shame. The American Army had never suffered such a trouncing. President Washington, himself a great military leader, vowed that Little Turtle's victory was not the end of the matter. Washington sent two of his bravest soldiers to negotiate a peace treaty with Little Turtle.

Col. John Hardin and Capt. Alexander Trueman were veterans of the American Revolution and had been fighting Indians in Kentucky and southern Ohio. An unfortunate choice for a peace expedition, Hardin was particularly hated and feared by the Shawnee. When the peace party arrived at the Miami camp, they were met with hostility.

Colonel Hardin was seized and killed immediately. Captain Trueman suffered an even more terrible fate. After being horribly tortured for hours, he was burned to death.

When news of the murder of the peace mission reached President Washington, he called for his old friend, Gen. Anthony Wayne.

Washington instructed Wayne to return to Kentucky and assemble an army capable of punishing and subduing the Indians. Orders were plain: "Drive the Indians out of Ohio."

General Wayne was widely known as "Mad" Anthony Wayne because he never accepted defeat. Under withering attack by the British during the Revolutionary War, he exposed himself to enemy fire to inspire his men in battle. He always led his men into battle, always at the front and in the thick of it, and his troops became as determined and as disciplined as he was. Wayne had proved himself to be a brilliant tactician, leading armies against the British and their Indian allies. He gave and expected no quarter—you would have to kill him to defeat him.

When Wayne arrived in Kentucky in 1792, he had his officer corps and a few regular army soldiers with him. He called on every able-bodied man to volunteer and recruited the best marksmen in Kentucky. Within two years, he had drilled and disciplined his men into a finely honed military machine. Every man learned that Wayne intended to fight to the death, and was willing to follow him into hell.

In the spring of 1794, General Wayne crossed the Ohio River with three thousand hardened veterans. As he marched up the banks of the Great Miami River, he destroyed every Indian camp and village he came across. His young lieutenant, William Henry Harrison, was learning the art of Indian warfare from the master. Little Turtle of the Miami and Blue Jacket of the Shawnee tried to slow Wayne's march with lightning attacks and skirmishes, but Wayne was always ready and always took control of the field.

Little Turtle and the Miami Confederation withdrew to regroup in northern Ohio along the Maumee River. Wayne built Fort Hamilton as an outpost and supply post that would securely hold his gains in southwestern Ohio. Moving up the Miami, he built Fort St. Clair (at modern-day Eaton) as a staging area for future attacks on the Indians and as a direct insult to Little Turtle's confederacy. Near St. Mary's he built Fort Recovery on the very site where General Butler had met his end—a symbol that he had recovered the territories St. Clair had lost.

Little Turtle made several attempts to overrun Anthony's camp at Fort Recovery. Each time he was soundly defeated. Little Turtle found that the British, who had previously supplied and armed the Indians, were no longer willing to join the fight. Some of the tribes that had supported the confederation had gone home after the first war.

Little Turtle also realized that this new general was of a different mettle than St. Clair, and Wayne's men were better armed and outnumbered the Miami and Shawnee. Like Chief Le Gris before him, Little Turtle began to argue for peace. General Wayne rejected peace talks and demanded that the Indians leave Ohio. Little Turtle counseled the confederation to accept Wayne's terms, but Blue Jacket (Shawnee) and Buckongahelas (Lenape) rejected Little Turtle's advice.

When Little Turtle refused to lead his Miami into a battle that he knew was already lost, Blue Jacket rose to leadership in the confederation. He drew the Lenape (Delaware), Mingo, Wyandot, Ottawa, Ojibwa, Potawatomi, and a few Miami into his camp. He began to organize his army of 1,500 warriors at a meadow that had been devastated by a tornado. Trees had fallen everywhere, affording plenty of cover. It would make a good place from which to fight.

In late July, Wayne marched his army in the Maumee Valley and built Fort Defiance. The name of the fort described his attitude. When a relief column bringing supplies was attacked, Wayne determined to end the war. The Indians customarily spent the days and nights before a battle in fasting, dancing, and praying. Wayne intentionally delayed his attack to allow hunger and fatigue to weaken his enemies. On the morning of August 20, 1794, he attacked.

The battle lasted only a few hours. By noon, it was all over. Wayne's troops simply overwhelmed the enemy. He sustained thirty-three killed and one hundred wounded. The Indian losses were relatively light too—just 240 dead—but hundreds were wounded. Blue Jacket's confederation crumbled. The Shawnee retreated to the British Fort Miami for protection. The other Indians laid down their weapons.

The Battle of Fallen Timbers was a decisive victory. Afterward, Wayne burned the Indians' crops and destroyed their villages, to further stress his defeated enemies. He treated the Indians as a conquered people, unwilling to make even the smallest concessions to them. He spent the next year at Fort Green Ville, forcing the Indians into accepting his terms in the Treaty of Green Ville. For little more than $20,000 in cash and trade goods (blankets, utensils, a few cattle and horses), the Indians gave up most of Ohio, Fort Detroit, northern Indiana, and the future site of Chicago. The Wyandots, under Chief Tarke, retreated into the Black Swamp, securing a twelve-square-mile reservation. Wayne allowed an additional ten square miles in northwestern Ohio for those other Indians who chose to stay.

The Miami moved west, first into Indiana and finally to Missouri and Kansas. The Ojibwa withdrew to Wisconsin and Minnesota. The Kickapoo, Wea, and Potawatomi tribes moved west of the Mississippi River. Blue Jacket and the Shawnee moved on into Canada and sought the aid of the British. A few Shawnee, including Tecumseh, refused to accept the treaty and went back home to the wild territories of south-central Ohio. There, they would prepare to join the British in the War of 1812.

RACCOONS BUILD A BOOKSHELF

1803

There was an important meeting under way in a little log cabin amidst the towering hardwood trees in hilly Athens County in fall 1803. Ohio had just been declared a state that year, and Athens County was still very much the frontier. Just four years earlier, the very first clearings had been hacked out of the forest for homes and garden plots. Now the settlers had gathered, traveling miles on foot or on the horses tethered outside, to discuss matters of urgent concern.

As historian Sarah Cutler wrote, "The sturdy men of this group, with bronzed faces and toil-worn hands, toughened . . . by wielding the ax and saw," came to this meeting "wearing their everyday home-spun and buckskin garments."

The first item on the agenda was improvement of the rough tracks loosely called roads in the area, so muddy in winter as to be almost impassable. The second was how they might manage to acquire something they felt a great lack of in their lives—books.

When listing the rock-bottom necessities of life, not everyone would include books—especially not, one might imagine, pioneers whose everyday lives were focused on urgent physical and practical necessities. But many of these settlers had come from New England and were no strangers to the comfort and value of the printed word. They wanted books to read by the fireside and candlelight; to enliven the long, dark winter nights; to help them learn things they needed to know; and, most of all, to educate the children already populating the scattered cabins of Athens County. The only reading material available to them now was outdated copies of a newspaper subscribed to by one of the settlers, reverently passed from hand to hand.

How they might acquire these earnestly wished-for volumes was a good question, however. Cash was scarce on the frontier—most of the everyday needs of life were obtained by barter. What little cash the settlers had was usually carefully hoarded to pay taxes or mortgages. One man who grew up in the area at the time said he never even saw a coin until he was a teenager.

Then one of the meeting attendees, Josiah True, had an idea. They might not have any money, but the forests and fields—still visited by Indians as a prime hunting ground—were full of wild game. Maybe they could hunt and trap their way to a collection of pelts that could be sold to buy books. The settlers knew how to work together to raise barns, piece quilts, and harvest crops—they could do this.

They left the meeting with a mission. All that winter, the woods and ravines rang out with rifle shots and the snap of steel traps as the men of Amesville and nearby settlements of Sunday Creek and Dover strove to fulfill that mission. There were some tense moments, such as the time Josiah True and another young man chased a bear into a cave and shot it. True was behind the bear, bending down to help push it out, when a second bear exploded from farther back in the cave and ran right over him, "crushing him down on his face with great violence" before it made its escape.

By spring, Samuel Brown and Ephraim Cutler of the settlement were loading a big wagon with furs: bear, wolf, fox, mink, a mountain lion and bobcat or two, and raccoons—lots of raccoons. They then made a strenuous six-hundred-mile journey over the mountains of Pennsylvania and on to Boston, where they sold their precious cargo for $74. Afterward, with the aid of two Boston residents, one of whom taught at Harvard, they thoughtfully selected fifty-one volumes to carry back to Ohio.

When those books finally reached Amesville on the back of a packhorse, they were lovingly unloaded. They formed the nucleus of a little library that was officially christened the Western Library Association, although most people just called it the Coonskin Library. This was not the first library in Ohio. A very small one had been founded in Belpre, not far from Marietta, in 1795 and one organized in Cincinnati in 1802 by Governor St. Clair and twenty-three other city residents. But the Coonskin Library was certainly one of the first, a true indication of Ohioans' respect for knowledge.

The Coonskin Library, like most other libraries of the day, was not the free public library we take for granted today. You had to be a subscriber to use the library (shares were $2.50 each) and pay yearly fees for maintenance. In this case, shares and yearly fees were sometimes paid in coonskins. The library rules were carefully codified, with stiff fines for things like fingerprints on pages; ripped, bent, or burned pages; or missing ones. If you were guilty of an overdue book, an appeals process could be invoked—a humane concept considering that one might have to ford swollen rivers or dodge Indian war parties to return a volume.

The original collection included encyclopedias, histories, and biographies; books on geography, philosophy, and religion (the books were chosen by two ministers); many works of the popular author Oliver Goldsmith; and even a few novels. Added in later years were subjects like Shakespeare's plays, poetry by Pope and Lord Byron, Bacon's essays, the life of Samuel Johnson, and Plutarch's *Lives.* Lord Byron, far away in London, is reported to have written in his diary, "These are the first tidings that have ever sounded like fame to my ears—to be read on the banks of the Ohio!"

After thirty-five years of hard use, the beloved Coonskin Library fell out of favor as reading materials from the East and elsewhere became more readily available. The remaining books were sold, finally ending up in the hands of Sarah Cutler, who was a direct descendant of those who created the little library. She eventually donated the collection to the Ohio Historical Society in Columbus, where it can be seen today.

In its heyday, the Coonskin Library was split into two branches. A smaller collection of books from the Dover branch are preserved at Ohio University. There is also a small museum in Amesville— founded in 1994 under the leadership of Gary Avery, a local school guidance counselor and Coonskin Library enthusiast—where you can see stuffed raccoons, coonskins, and a few sample books from the library.

Ohio's interest in libraries didn't stop here. The state library was founded in 1817, and by 1850 there were 187 "subscription" libraries like the Coonskin in the state. The first free public library west of the Appalachians—the Lane Library in Hamilton, Ohio—was instituted in 1866, and the first-ever free county library system in the United States was created in Van Wert County after John S. Brumback's generous gift of a building to hold it. In the late nineteenth and early twentieth centuries, with the aid of the deep pockets of Andrew Carnegie, 111 public libraries were added to Ohio. In later years, politicians like William Howard Taft and Governor Richard Celeste made sure that the state provided support for those stacks, card catalogs, reading rooms, and library computer stations stretched across Ohio.

Thanks to these efforts, in 2002 a national survey indicated that Ohio's libraries were the best in the country, both as a whole and in the individual excellence of a number of specific ones. Beginning in the 1960s, Ohio added to its distinctions by creating Ohiolink, the country's first statewide computer network of libraries and electronic information sources, bringing together the resources of eighty-four Ohio colleges and universities plus the State Library of Ohio.

In addition to its public library system, the state has more than a hundred specialty libraries, including the Black Heritage and Multicultural Center in Findlay; the First Ladies' Library in Canton, founded by the wife of President McKinley; the NASA Glenn Research Center in Cleveland, focusing on aeronautical subjects and space; Cincinnati's history-filled Mercantile Library; the eye-opening collection of football memorabilia at the Professional Football Hall of Fame in Canton; and the Ohioana Library, a unique library in Columbus devoted exclusively to the creative output of Ohio writers and songwriters.

The book lovers of early Amesville would be proud.

THE GREAT APPLE PLANTER
ARRIVES IN OHIO

1806

There may have been stranger sights on the highway in Jefferson County, but this was still a strange one. The highway, as in most of Ohio at the turn of the nineteenth century, was not a blacktopped or concrete road but a waterway—in this case, the broad Ohio River in the spring of 1806.

Two canoes lashed together were headed downstream, powered by the furious paddling of a gaunt, oddly dressed man with long, dark hair, a scruffy beard, and peculiar headgear. Snuggled into those canoes were leather bags packed with apple seeds—360,000 per bushel. John Chapman, aka Johnny Appleseed, was getting serious about Ohio. He'd done a few plantings in the state in 1800 and was now headed for the Muskingum Valley in north-central Ohio. This was not the region of peaceful rolling farmland, small towns, and the occasional small city it is now but a wild and wooly part of the country's western frontier.

Johnny Appleseed is one of our favorite American folk heroes. Songs, stories, festivals, and books about him abound—to the point that it is sometimes hard to separate fact from fiction. But he was a real person. Born in Leominster, Massachusetts, as John Chapman, he was the son of a farmer, carpenter, and soldier in the Continental Army. As a boy, John was apprenticed to a neighboring farmer who had orchards, and by the age of eighteen he took off for Pennsylvania to start his eccentric travels and unusual trade. After a dozen years of practice among the pioneers in the hills of western Pennsylvania, he followed the wave of settlement to Ohio, where he spent the majority of his long career as (in his own words) "a gatherer and planter of apple seeds."

He didn't just wander from place to place sticking those seeds in the ground as a purely altruistic undertaking. This was a carefully worked-out business. First he obtained the seeds by patiently picking them out of the pomace—mashed pulp—left over when a mill pressed apples into cider. He then toted the seeds to the places he expected the westward push to go next and set up crude little nurseries. This meant finding a fertile spot, girdling a few trees, planting some seeds, and building a little brush fence around the plot. By the time settlers arrived in that area in force a couple of years later, there would be sturdy little apple seedlings ready for sale or barter. By then Johnny would have moved on, but before he did, he arranged for others in the area to sell the seedlings for him when they were ready.

Johnny wasn't just providing these early pioneers with a handsome landscape tree or source of something to toss into a lunch bag or present to the teacher. Apples were a household staple for pioneer Americans, a hardy fruit of a hundred uses. They were not merely eaten fresh but also dried, stewed, and made into apple butter and applesauce. Apples became cider, hard cider, apple brandy, vinegar, and feed for cattle. They could be stored in the cellar over the winter to help keep the family healthy in the months when few other fresh foods were available, and they could be bartered for other staples. Some homestead laws even required settlers to have a stand of apple trees as a condition of keeping the land they had traveled far, struggled, and sometimes fought to gain.

Being well aware of all of this, Johnny was generous with his apple trees. If a settler didn't have the money to pay for them (the going price was about 6 cents apiece) or anything to exchange for them, John would take IOUs or just make a gift of them. One time near Mansfield, Ohio, he encountered a family of nine orphaned children struggling to get by and gave them sixty young trees to start an orchard.

Johnny didn't just bring apples to the rough-and-tumble Ohio frontier—dense forests and fields full of people doing just about anything they had to do to survive and make a living. A thoughtful and gentle man, he brought an example of kindness, tolerance, and compassion for all creatures, not just fellow humans. This made him really stand out in an area and time when most people believed that the only good Indian was a dead one and wolves and bears were animals to be disposed of as quickly as possible. His constant travels brought him into frequent contact with Indians, who respected him for his knowledge of plants and wildlife, his courage and stoicism, and the fact that he was as at home in the woods and wilds as they were.

Though Johnny generally worked to make whites more aware of the rights and respect due Indians, there was one time when he lent the settlers a helping hand in Indian matters. In September 1812, after war was declared between the United States and Great Britain (and their Indian allies), the settlers in the area of Mount Vernon and Mansfield viewed all Indians pretty nervously. They persuaded the inhabitants of the Indian town of Greentown to move out "temporarily" for their own safety; as soon as the Indians left, renegade soldiers torched the town. In Mansfield all the Indians were gathered up and put under guard. When one harmless old Wyandot attempted to escape with his young daughter, he was killed, scalped, and beheaded, and his head was stuck on a pole in town.

Needless to say, Indian war parties followed. A local trader was killed and scalped, and two men who had been working nearby went missing. All the local soldiers were off with the Greentown Indians, so the white families in the immediate area ran for the blockhouse. But a warning needed to go out to Mansfield and outlying areas and reinforcements summoned.

Johnny Appleseed volunteered to sound the alarm. Many accounts have him doing this barefoot in the moonlight, running the thirty miles from Mansfield to Mount Vernon, blowing a powder horn and crying, "Flee for your lives; the British and Indians are coming." More prosaic historians feel it was more likely done on horseback, since speed was of the essence.

Some records have him saying, a little more poetically, ". . . the Lord hath appointed me to blow the trumpet in the wilderness and sound an alarm in the forest, for behold, the tribes of the heathen are round your doors, and a devouring flame followeth after them." What he said and how he traveled may be disputed, but he did make the trip.

It's been estimated that Johnny Appleseed planted trees over one hundred thousand square miles in his lifetime. One tree that Johnny himself planted survives in Nova, Ohio, a little above Ashland. Having been set in the ground when Andrew Jackson was president, it is 170 years old, and you can have a part of it. The American Forests Famous and Historic Trees Project offers cuttings grafted to semi-dwarf or dwarf rootstocks.

Although Johnny did not approve of grafted trees, this is a fine green apple. As the organization's literature says, "Here is a chance to sink your teeth into a piece of American history."

"WE HAVE MET THE ENEMY, AND THEY ARE OURS"

1813

On September 10, 1813, a young American naval officer led his hastily built fleet of nine small ships out of Put-in-Bay on Lake Erie to confront the British squadron that controlled the Great Lakes. Under the command of Robert Heriot Barclay, a decorated veteran of England's smashing defeat of the French and Spanish forces at Trafalgar, this small but formidable British fleet controlled America's inland waterways just as the main English fleet had ruled the high seas since 1600.

When the smoke cleared on this day, however, the British fleet had suffered the most humiliating naval loss in its history, and Commodore Oliver Hazard Perry had become the "Hero of Lake Erie."

After Gen. William Henry Harrison drove the Indians out of Ohio in 1811, they allied with the British in Canada. When the United States and Britain went to war in 1812, British sea power had secured control of the Great Lakes. They were able to transport their Indian allies by ship to attack the Americans all along the coast of the lakes. Their grip on the Great Lakes also allowed them to supply their armies in Canada and along the northern coast of Ohio, Pennsylvania, and New York. The Americans had to win Lake Erie or lose the war.

Oliver Hazard Perry joined the U.S. Navy when he was only twelve years old, serving on his father's ship. Before he was fifteen, he was a veteran of several naval battles. During the Barbary Wars in the Mediterranean, he commanded the USS *Nautilus.* In late 1812 Secretary of the Navy Paul Hamilton had ordered the creation of a secret shipbuilding facility at Presque Isle (French for "almost an island") on the coast of what is now Erie, Pennsylvania.

In February 1813 the youthful Commander Perry boldly claimed the office of Commander of the Great Lakes and the job of supervising the construction of an American fleet there. In nearly record time, he constructed two brigs in his concealed Presque Isle shipyard.

This feat was accomplished with very few experienced boatwrights. Perry had recruited semiskilled men from Pittsburgh and Philadelphia as well as a few real sailors to work in the shipyard. Many of the laborers were free blacks from Ohio. Since there were almost no nails available, the shipbuilders had to pound wooden pegs into the green, fresh-cut lumber. The ships' armament was cast-iron carronades—short, smoothbore cannons. They were powerful but short ranged. In close combat, they could rake the enemy's deck with three hundred pounds of grapeshot, disabling the masts, ripping sails, and bloodying sailors.

As his ships progressed, Perry also commandeered four merchant ships and pressed them into service. They were refitted with cannons from the foundry at Frenchtown before the British could seize the foundry. The U.S. Army had captured the *Caledonia* in October 1812 and commandeered the schooners *Ohio, Somers,* and *Trippe,* which they moved to Black Rock to refit as gunboats—small, fast-attack ships.

Barclay discovered the hidden shipworks at Black Rock but couldn't get his heavy gunships across the shoals protecting the harbor. When Barclay briefly lifted the siege, Perry used oxen to drag the boats up the Niagara River to Lake Erie, where he sailed them into his secret shipworks at Presque Isle.

When Barclay finally stumbled upon the Presque Isle shipyard, he found it heavily defended by Pennsylvania militia and heavy cannons. He retired with his fleet to the eastern end of Lake Erie, trying to intercept the Black Rock ship movement but missing them. The boats had already made their way to Perry.

Perry believed he had been born for this war. Even his middle name, Hazard, was a portent of his destiny and willingness to fight against great odds. He patiently waited for Barclay's squadron to run short of supplies. That forced Barclay to lift the siege of Presque Isle in July long enough for Perry to lead his force onto the lake. Perry anchored his ships at Put-in-Bay and for the next five weeks drilled his sailors in use of the carronades and in discipline under fire.

When the morning of September 10, 1813, dawned, he was ready to engage the enemy.

The wind shifted that morning, pushing Barclay's ships away from the bay, and Perry took advantage of the shift to get his ships to sea. At a distance, he spotted Barclay's flagship, the *Detroit*. Barclay's squadron included the brigs HMS *Queen Charlotte* and HMS *Lady Prevost*, as well as the *Hunter*, *Little Belt*, and HMS *Chippewa*.

By themselves, Perry's two brigs, *Niagara* and the *Lawrence*, were no match for the *Detroit* and its battle-hardened crew, but he made up for it with the speed of his gunboat-rigged schooners. The schooners USS *Scorpion* and *Aries*, along with the *Tigress* and *Porcupine*, were dispatched to dart in among the heavy British ships, fire on the

the masts and crews, and then retire while the *Lawrence* and *Niagara* engaged them in mortal combat.

The success of the gunboats became obvious when the masts of both the *Charlotte* and the *Detroit* were damaged, causing the loss of their ability to steer and maneuver. They still had big guns that wreaked havoc on the *Lawrence,* forcing Perry to move his battle flag to the *Niagara.* The *Lawrence* had been named for Perry's friend, Capt. James Lawrence, whose dying words had been "Don't give up the ship." Perry had commissioned a blue-and-white flag with that motto to serve as his command flag. As he climbed into a longboat to transfer his command to *Niagara,* he stood in the bow wrapped in that flag. The inspiration of seeing their commander erect and still full of fight gave his men the will to finish the task before them.

Before the *Detroit* and *Charlotte* could move in to finish off the *Lawrence,* the winds shifted again. Unable to maneuver, the *Charlotte* and *Detroit* got their masts entangled. Seizing the opportunity, Perry brought *Niagara* in close and raked the deck of both ships with his carronades. With the great British warships disabled and their smaller vessels captured, the *Detroit* struck her flag. Barclay, lying mortally wounded, surrendered his command.

In a little over four hours, Commodore Perry, having just turned twenty-eight years old, had defeated the greatest naval power on Earth. The Americans had won control of the Great Lakes, and the British army could no longer threaten the interior of the United States.

Perry lost twenty-seven men and had ninety-six wounded. But he had captured 306 British sailors; killed forty-one, including all the officers; and wounded ninety-three. The defeat of the mighty Britannia reverberated around the world. The myth of English invincibility on the waves was shattered.

After the battle, Perry sent a message to Gen. William Henry Harrison: "We have met the enemy, and they are ours—two ships, two brigs, one schooner, and one sloop." Perry had captured the entire British Great Lakes fleet.

Perry's triumphant message assured General Harrison of victory in his own endeavor. Harrison was chasing the British army across Canada. Unable to be resupplied because of Perry's victory, the British generals ordered a hasty retreat under fire. Perry landed troops behind the British lines, leaving them nowhere to run.

The combination of Perry's victory on Lake Erie and Harrison's subsequent success in Canada assured the place of the United States as a world power.

Today the Perry Victory and International Peace Memorial stands on the longest undefended international border in the world at South Bass Island, a short ferry ride from Put-in-Bay. Three American and three British officers are interred there. In the visitor center stands a statue created in 1860 by Ohio-born sculptor William Walcutt. The massive 352-foot-tall Doric column that dominates the memorial is the fourth tallest monument in the United States. The Peace Memorial is a fitting symbol of the friendship of the United States and Canada (and, indeed, Great Britain), which has endured now for two centuries.

THE GREAT GROUNDBREAKING

1825

In Licking County, almost the dead center of the state, July fourth was usually one of the most celebrated days of the year. But this particular Independence Day, which dawned bright and sunny in 1825, was a very special one. A high spot in the county, then called Licking Summit, about three miles south of Newark, had been chosen for the Great Groundbreaking. Here the fledgling state of Ohio would boldly begin one of the most ambitious—and backbreaking—public works ever undertaken anywhere, innocuously known as the Ohio Canal System.

"It seems almost a miracle that a state in its infancy should undertake and create so great a work," noted Senator John C. Calhoun of South Carolina.

To create this marvel of the age, more than 740 million cubic feet of soil would be dug up and moved—not by trackhoe or backhoe or bulldozer, but by pick and shovel and wheelbarrow. Countless thousands of tons of rock would be quarried and moved for this same purpose. When this new waterway network was complete—one

thousand miles counting all its branches—a couple of mules plod-
ding down a dirt path with a single rope would be able to pull a sixty-
foot boat loaded with up to eighty tons of cargo, without benefit of
a motor. And Ohioans across the state would finally have a way to
reach markets for the ever-multiplying products of their hard work
and rich soil.

Although this shining vision was still a couple of years in the
future, July 4, 1825, was the day it would all be set in motion. Thou-
sands of Ohioans from almost every county, rough and ready citizens
and the more refined, had gathered here in anticipation, and the inns
of the area were filled to bursting.

The guest of honor for the event would be the tall, handsome
governor of New York State, DeWitt Clinton. As one more indica-
tion of why this new transportation system was badly needed, Clin-
ton had left Albany by stagecoach in June in order to be here in time
for the event, and his traveling companions had been two Eastern
financiers who were helping make this project possible by lending
Ohio the money to fund it, in this case at 5 percent interest.

Clinton was the obvious choice for the figurehead of the day, a
perfect prophet for spreading canal fever. Only recently completed,
the Erie Canal, which he had championed for New York State, had
turned New York City into the leading seaport in the nation and
transformed Buffalo from a sleepy village of two hundred souls to a
small city of eighteen thousand and growing madly. The Erie Canal
was also transporting a steady stream of immigrants from all over the
world, heading for Ohio.

A cavalcade of coaches, carriages, and colorful troops of Ohio
cavalry, artillery, and infantry met Clinton at Newark, where he had
arrived the night before, and escorted him to the newly constructed
grandstand at the summit. Then those foot soldiers and mounted
men with their stamping horses (the horseflies were ferocious after

three previous days of rain) surrounded the speakers' stand so tightly that few of the massed citizens were able to hear all the grand rhetoric that followed—the speeches of Clinton, Ohio Governor Jeremiah Morrow, and Tom Ewing of Lancaster—or the blessing of the preacher. But the mood of the day was exuberant, and each speaker was rewarded with enthusiastic shouts and cheers.

The assemblage then moved to the actual site of the ground-breaking. Clinton sank a spade into the clay of Ohio, followed by Governor Morrow, a farmer as well as statesman, who obviously had more experience with this sturdy, sticky stuff. Spadefuls by other attending notables followed, including the captain of the honor guard of Chillicothe Blues and even those New York bankers.

When the ceremonial wheelbarrow was full, it was trucked up to the canal bank-to-be and upended. As author N. N. Hill Jr. noted in *A History of Licking County,* "It is impossible to describe the . . . excitement and confusion that accompanied this ceremony. The people shouted themselves hoarse . . . tears fell from many eyes."

All then retired to long tables made from freshly sawn lumber set out nearby, where a feast prepared by an innkeeper from Lancaster was spread out (for a mere $1.50 a head!). Many toasts were proposed and drunk to everyone and everything from Washington and Jefferson, who first imagined American canals, to the present company and the glorious future. Each toast was accompanied by a blast of artillery until the powder finally gave out—but not the liquor.

For the locals, one of the reasons for all this celebrating was the fact that the canal would be going through here. When the Ohio legislature finally approved the construction of two canals in the state in February 1825, the engineer who masterminded the Erie Canal surveyed possible routes for canals in Ohio.

He recommended five possible routes, but far more than geography, topography, availability of water sources to keep the canals filled, and the flow patterns of the rivers and streams with regard to the Continental Divide had to be taken into account. There was also that inescapable factor known as self-interest—all in favor of the canals wanted to be directly on their route to be in the best position to reap the advantages. Much creative lobbying and juggling followed.

The promoters of a future Akron, for example, threw a free canal right-of-way and one third of the prospective town lots into the kitty in an attempt to lure the route their way; they succeeded. Likewise, the developer of Waverly, in south-central Ohio, offered to finance a road and bridge and build a courthouse should the canal go that way instead of via Piketon; oddly enough, it did.

The two routes that were finally chosen—the Ohio and Erie Canal on the eastern side of the state and the Miami and Erie Canal in the west—were in the end political and hydrologic compromises. But they would achieve the objective of linking Ohio's two major bodies of water, the Ohio River and Lake Erie, so that the state's wheat, corn, pork, lumber, whiskey, wool, tobacco, and many other products no longer needed to be flatboated all the way to New Orleans.

And those canals were built—speedily, considering the challenges. Many thousands of Irish and German immigrants, Ohio farm boys, and here and there a few Ohio prisoners put their shoulders to pick and shovel and to driving the teams of horses and oxen that pulled the wagons to dig those forty-foot-wide, four-foot-deep channels and build the locks that enabled boats to be raised or lowered as necessary to navigate the waterways. They chipped and cut their way through hills and valleys, swamps and forests, for 30¾ cents a day, plus (at least in the beginning) four jiggers of whiskey a day to ward off the chills and fever of malaria, cholera, and other scourges of the undertaking.

The total cost of the canal system, counting all that interest to the Eastern bankers, was $41 million. But it was a bargain for the young state of Ohio. It not only gave anyone in the state (not just those who happened to live on the Ohio River or one of its major tributaries) access to national markets for the first time—and a much better return on its agricultural production—but also upped the value of land along the canals, and all of Ohio, by ten times or more.

The canal system more than doubled the population of the state, laid the foundation for industry along the canal routes, and was the initiator and developer of many of Ohio's most prosperous towns and cities today.

True, the expensive and extensive canal system had a mere twenty-five years of vigorous life before it was made obsolete by a much less limited form of transport, the railroad. But in its short span, the canal system enabled Ohio to make a giant step toward self-realization and national prominence.

So go visit the remains of this impressive network now and enjoy the ambience of a slower and gentler time. Many parts and pieces of the canal system remain, where you can hike, bike, or ride a canal boat down a stretch of canal or even through one of the few remaining working locks.

TROUBLED BRIDGES OVER
THE WATERS

1835

The Wells Fargo stagecoach traveling from Pittsburgh to Columbus was making very good time. All four horses were running well, everyone was rested from a good night's sleep in Pittsburgh, and with any luck the passengers would be in Columbus in two days. After the mail drop-off in Norwich, the coach headed out of town, downhill toward the Muskingum River.

The National Road had made travel fast and mostly safe. But this coachman was a new driver and unfamiliar with the road and the strange bridge ahead, one of Ohio's five S-shaped stone-arch bridges. He was going too fast when he hit the curves. The coach pitched first to the left and then swung wildly to the right as it flipped over, tossing the driver and coachman over the stone wall and into the river below.

The two trailing horses suffered broken hindquarters as the tongue of the coach broke loose and rode up over them. They had to be put down.

The coach tumbled to a jolting stop against the stone walls of the bridge, and the injured passengers crawled out. A woman with a broken arm and her son, badly bruised but alive, scrambled away from the wreck.

Then there was Christopher C. Baldwin, a librarian from Boston on his way to Columbus to meet with state education officials. On August 20, 1835, on the curves of the "S" bridge just outside Norwich, Mr. Baldwin, his neck broken, became Ohio's first recorded traffic fatality. It was the first of many such accidents on Ohio's "alphabet bridges."

Ohio is home to some of the most unusual bridges in the world. They are often called alphabet bridges because they are in the shape of letters of the alphabet, "S" and "Y" in particular.

In 1806 President Jefferson became convinced of the need to tie the newly opened interior of the country to the eastern seaboard. Attempts had already been made to separate the new territories west of the Allegheny and Smoky Mountains from the United States, but the people of the West wanted to be part of the country. Jefferson's political party had opposed the use of federal government money on internal improvement projects, but he clearly saw the necessity of it. He urged Congress to appropriate money to build a National Road.

By 1811 the construction had begun. It followed the trail of the Cumberland Road, the path most used by settlers moving from the coast into the Northwest Territory. Road construction progressed from Baltimore to present-day Wheeling, West Virginia, until the War of 1812 brought construction to a halt. After the war, the clamor of settlers for better access to Ohio and points west forced Congress to renew its commitment to building the National Road. By 1825 the road had been completed across ten Ohio counties and continued into Indiana, eventually reaching St. Louis on the Mississippi.

Ohio posed a whole new set of engineering challenges. Due to the patterns of glaciation, Ohio's rivers don't all run in the same direction. The road was laid out, the trail cut through the dense forests of central Ohio, but the rivers weren't cooperating. Some rivers converged into other rivers right where the road was supposed to cross. Other rivers made meandering turns where the road was laid. A solution, unique to Ohio, had to be found.

The first problem was just up the road from Wheeling at Bridgeport, Ohio. The bends and turns in the river posed a challenge. The bridge would have to cross Wheeling Creek and then the Ohio River if the two banks were to be linked. Engineers decided that the answer was to continue building the road on opposite sides of the river and to build ramps for a bridge at the most suitable places where they could create a right angle. Since those places were significantly offset at angles from each other because of the way the rivers meandered, a device for creating a 90-degree angle across the waters had to be invented. The answer was to build the bridge in the shape of an "S."

The Blaine Hill Bridge at Bridgeport had to traverse 345 feet of water and then proceed uphill at a 6.3 percent angle. To achieve this engineering feat, they decided to use stone arches. Stone was stronger and more permanent than wood. The engineers calculated that construction could be accomplished with three arches. Then the road could be laid atop the arches.

Construction began in 1828 on the first federally funded bridge on the National Highway. The "S" bridge at Blaine Hill is the longest bridge of its type in America. Viewed from above, it appears to be shaped like an "S." According to legend, the "S" shape was supposed to slow down runaway horse and wagon teams, but it was the perverse nature of Ohio's rivers that made it necessary and the genius of the engineers that made it possible. The National Road is now US 40 and is often called "America's Main Street."

The "S" bridge at Blaine Hill was the first of five such bridges constructed in Ohio. Four more such bridges were built in Guernsey County, crossing creek after creek. The "S" bridges served their purpose through the horse-and-buggy age and into the automotive era. When automobile speeds became a safety issue, most of the "S" bridges were straightened and reconstructed. The S-shaped bridge at Blaine Hill and four others remain accessible to public traffic, but new steel spans have been built to carry the high-speed traffic on new highways.

Muskingum County needed a different solution to its problem. At Zanesville, the Licking River and two branches of the Muskingum River converged right in the middle of town, splitting the city into three different communities. If the National Road ever made it to Zanesville, an imaginative answer was required to solve the crossover problem and to unite the city. The city fathers clearly saw the problem—and the solution. Why not build a Y-shaped bridge to unite the three sections of Zanesville?

It had never been done before, but engineers took up the challenge. In 1814 the first "Y" bridge, a covered bridge, was constructed of wooden piles and a wooden deck that spanned the rivers. The problem with wooden bridges, even covered ones, was that they were prone to catch fire. After reconstructing the bridge a fourth time, the city fathers sought a more permanent solution in the mid-nineteenth century.

Using elements of the same stone-arch construction technology that earlier had been used so well in the "S" bridges, they began building ramps from three different directions. Over each river branch they constructed new arches, connecting them when they reached the middle of the rivers. Today the fifth "Y" bridge at Zanesville is a sandstone, steel, and concrete span that opened in 1984. It has become a tourist attraction in its own right. Locals love to give directions to visitors saying, "Go to the middle of the bridge and turn right."

The Zanesville "Y" bridge proved to be a creative answer to a vexing problem, and it provided the answer to a similar problem at Akron a century later. In 1981 Memorial Bridge, a steel-girder span carrying OH 261, was constructed over the Little Cuyahoga River. In the middle of the river, the four lanes split into two two-lane pairs. The bridge has been renamed the All-American Bridge.

The unique S- and Y-shaped bridges of Ohio, still in use today, are listed on the National Registry of Historic Places.

ON THIN ICE

1838

It was late February 1838, and one of the two and a half million blacks in slavery in "the Land of the Free"—these United States—had made a decision. She was going to try to escape north, perhaps with the help of that shadowy network whispered about on the slave grapevine that would come to be known as the Underground Railroad.

The farm she lived on was in Dover, Kentucky, from which you could almost toss a flat rock and see it skip across the surface of the broad Ohio River. That storied river, the dividing line between North and South, had more than four hundred miles of frontage in Ohio to tempt adventurous—or desperate—blacks to try to make it across to the other side.

We can't add "and thus freedom," because the Fugitive Slave Act and later amendments to it, passed to placate slave-owning states, meant that a runaway slave arriving in Ohio or any other Northern state would have to make it from there all the way to Canada before he or she would truly be free. But of the states bordering the South,

Ohio was the shortest—only 210 miles deep—so the trip through it to Lake Erie, and then on to Canada, was not impossible.

The heroine of our story was going to see if she could do it. The decision had really been made for her. Her owners, the Davis family, had not subjected her to any of the extraordinary cruelties that other slaveholders had been known to inflict on their charges, but they had fallen into financial difficulties. As a result, her bright and lively two-year-old son—she had lost two children earlier—would be separated from her tomorrow and sold to the highest bidder. So late that night, she grabbed her son and headed for the river.

The nearest town on the Ohio side was Ripley, a bustling, irreverent little city that made much of its living off the traffic on the Ohio. Steamboats and flatboats hustled to and fro with cargoes and deliveries, including many a bale of tobacco and barrel of pork, for Ripley had tobacco warehouses and was the second-biggest pork-processing center after Cincinnati. But two additional things made Ripley a name that resounds in the history of the Underground Railroad: The river was relatively narrow and shallow here, and the town's inhabitants included a fair number of people willing to risk censure, violence, and imprisonment to lend a hand to slaves fleeing northward.

Our heroine may not have known all of this, but she'd heard that the Ohio River had been frozen over for the past week. When she finally reached the shore, however, it was clear that the ice was melting. A kindly white man on the Kentucky side gave her food and a chance to rest while she figured out what to do. He warned her that the river was no longer a slick, sturdy highway to deliverance but a death trap.

He was still trying to talk her out of attempting to cross when the sound of the slave catchers' dog pack reached their ears. She bolted for the door as he quickly wrapped her child in a woolen shawl and pulled a long wooden rail off his fence to aid her in her journey.

Just before the dogs reached her, she jumped onto the ice and headed for Ohio. The ice cracked and groaned and broke beneath her feet as she scrambled to secure a place for herself and her son on the bigger floating pieces. Leaping from floe to floe as best she could, she was soon soaked with freezing water. The fence rail saved her from sinking several times as she shunted the small body of her son ahead of her on the ice slabs. When she finally reached the other side, both she and her shivering child cried out in fear and exhaustion.

Ironically, this is what saved them. The river crossings—especially when iced over—were zealously watched by slave catchers and bounty hunters. This night was no exception. A sometime slave catcher by the name of Chancey Shaw had heard the commotion of her crossing. But he was so moved by her courage that he said, "Any woman who crossed that river carrying her baby has won her freedom." He helped our heroine to her feet, scurried through Ripley with her, and pointed her toward a redbrick house on a hill near the edge of town.

Once she climbed the steep wooden steps up that hill, she was at the home of John Rankin, a Presbyterian minister and ardent abolitionist. Rankin's "Letters on Slavery" (written to a brother who had bought some slaves) were printed in the local paper and eventually made into a book that became required reading for the antislavery movement across the country. During their forty years in Ripley, Rankin and his large family helped more than two thousand escapees from slavery.

Soon our heroine and her child were warm and dry and on their way to several of the numerous other "stations" by which slaves were spirited away and sheltered on the often-circuitous route to Canada.

In this case, one of the stations was the home of Levi Coffin, another very influential figure, often called the president of the Underground Railroad. Levi's wife gave our heroine the name Eliza Harris, and if that name and the story above sound somewhat familiar, it is because this is the real-life story upon which the most dramatic episode in *Uncle Tom's Cabin* was based—the book President Lincoln said (not entirely facetiously) had started the Civil War.

The Eliza-crossing-the-ice chapter of *Uncle Tom's Cabin* has even been called the most memorable passage in all of nineteenth-century literature. The real-life Eliza was short, plump, and dark, while Stowe's Eliza was light, lissome, and lovely. But then as now, show business is show business, and all is fair in love and the quest to win readers.

The real-life Eliza eventually reached Canada and settled in Chatham, Ontario. Amazingly enough, three years later she reappeared at Rankin's home while he was hoeing his garden and announced that she had returned to rescue the rest of her children (some accounts say her daughter and grandchildren). With the help of a crafty Americanized Canadian, she succeeded in doing so, although the undertaking was made more difficult by the daughter's insistence on carrying out not just the children but also several hundred pounds of personal possessions that she was loathe to leave behind.

Today the Rankin House (complete with a reconstruction of those wooden stairs) is a National Historic Landmark.

The Freedom Center in Cincinnati, which the *Chicago Tribune* called the one museum you need to see in Cincinnati if you see only one, is full of information and other dramatic stories about the Underground Railroad.

One of those stories is that of Margaret Garner. Margaret, a slave mother who escaped to Cincinnati and was recaptured there by slave hunters, killed her daughter and tried to kill her other children rather than see them returned to servitude. The State of Ohio tried to charge her with murder in hopes of keeping her (and then quietly releasing her), but the slaveholders invoked the Fugitive Slave Act.

Margaret was returned to slavery in the South, where she died of typhoid fever on a plantation in Mississippi.

THE GRIM FATE OF THE *GRIFFITH*

1850

One of the many steamships plying the Great Lakes in the mid-nineteenth century, the *G. P. Griffith* was a handsome one. Only three years old on this June night in 1850, she had two big paddle wheels, a dark brown hull, red-trimmed white upperworks, and trim black stacks. Her deck, twenty-eight feet wide and almost two hundred feet long, was filled from edge to edge with one of the most profitable cargos in the business—immigrants from "the old countries" on their way to new homes and farms in the Midwest.

As the passengers did their best to get comfortable for the night, without beds or cots or in many cases even bedding, you could hear the accents of the places they'd left behind weeks or even months ago on their way to America—Germany, Ireland, England, and Scandinavia. This might not be a luxurious voyage, but it was an easy two- or three-day jaunt compared to what it had taken them to get to this point.

Most of them had endured long voyages across the ocean in dirty, overcrowded, disease-ridden, and poorly provisioned ships.

After an unsettling arrival in New York or Boston, they had made overland and canal-boat journeys to Buffalo. And now they had reached the last leg of their journeys—this trip across Lake Erie to Toledo or Cleveland, where if they were lucky friends or family would help them get settled and make their way in this new world.

Although Lake Erie can be more dangerous than any ocean because of how quickly its shallow waters can be whipped up by winds that have nothing in the surrounding flat landscape to stop them, this was a calm and clear evening. But at 3:30 a.m., when the *Griffith* was traveling along smoothly just twenty miles east of Cleveland, the mate saw smoke billowing up from the hold and then a shower of sparks from between the stacks. Since the ship was only about three miles from the shore, the captain made a bold move. He turned the ship, full speed ahead, toward the shore. This would fan the flames, but they would reach land in five minutes or less.

Alas, when the *Griffith* was less than a thousand feet from land, it struck a sandbar and was grounded. The passengers, who had been fairly calm when the alarm first sounded and it seemed that a solution was at hand, panicked as flames now spread wildly and engulfed the ship.

Many of the forty or so first-class passengers were trapped in their cabins while the hordes of frantic deck passengers had to make a sudden choice between burning to death or jumping overboard. Curses, entreaties, and screams rang out. Families and couples held hands, muttered a prayer, and jumped. There were no lifeboats launched, no life preservers available. Even the captain threw his wife, children, and mother overboard before jumping over the side himself.

Some who dived overboard were crushed by the still-turning paddle wheels, but most hung in the water, crying out, thrashing, and struggling to stay alive and afloat. Few were strong swimmers, and many could not swim at all. So although the water was not cold and the shore was a mere seven hundred feet away, in less than half an hour, 295 of the 326 passengers were dead—drowned or burned to death. This included every child and all but one of the women aboard—boys and girls, wives and mothers and sisters looking forward to life in a new land. Many of the women had gold coins and other valuables sewn into their skirts and petticoats, and many of the men wore money belts. These carefully hoarded treasures to help fund that new life only helped doom them with added weight in the water.

When searchers went to retrieve the bodies, many were gripped together so tightly they could scarcely be separated, so desperately had they clung to one another in the waves. Some of the bodies were never recovered, and some were carried off by ships to other cities or shipped back to the Old Country. But even so, about a hundred of the dead were left on the shore, lined up in grim rows.

June 17, 1850, was an unusually hot day, so the need for burial was urgent. A committee of local citizens decided that a mass grave, right on the spot, was the answer. A long trench was dug on a knoll a little ways back from the beach, and the men, women, and children were piled in without shrouds, coffins, or headstones—without even names. Since the ship's books were lost, no one even knew who most of the victims were.

The notebook of the Lake County Commissioner of Wrecks noted many of the sad little traces of the victims' lives that were found later: "a blue frock coat, 2 pair of woolen pants, 13 pocket-knives, a pocket flask, 13 bonnets, 2 miniature portraits, a boy's book with his name inscribed on the flyleaf, 2 Catholic prayer books, 1 fiddle bow." Let us not contemplate what happened to all that gold and those money belts.

In later years the unmarked site was part of the picnic grounds of an amusement park, and the site was eventually destroyed by erosion of the shoreline. In 2000 a memorial marker was finally erected in the area, in the Lakefront Lodge Park of the city of Willowick.

The fiery destruction of the *Griffith* was the third worst disaster that ever occurred on the Great Lakes, and we are talking about bodies of fresh water that have claimed (depending on whose estimate you go with) between four and ten thousand ships over time. The cause of the fire was never determined, although speculations ranged from the new type of oil that was being used on this trip to the matches that made up part of its cargo, paint stored near the firebox, a defect in the water jacket in the fire hold, perhaps even a drunken crew member careless with matches.

The *Griffith* burned to the waterline, and what is left of the ship now lies on a rock-strewn sandy bottom in about thirty feet of water. In 1974 divers recovered the *Griffith*'s inscribed three-hundred-pound bell.

Something positive did come out of this tragedy. The horror of the event, which was only one of several fires and explosions on Great Lakes steamships that year, spurred studies and committees that resulted in the first-ever safety regulations for vessels on the Great Lakes, including regular inspections. Condemning the lack of safety provisions on the steamboats of the day, the report of the Committee of the Citizens of Cleveland in Relation to Steamboat Disasters on the Western Lakes noted: "Does not such recklessness involve the guilt of murder, and shall we make no effort to stay it?"

WEST POINT OR A PONY?

1861

Gilbert Van Zandt was not your typical hero. Born on December 20, 1851, in Port William, Ohio, "Lil' Gib," as the family called him, loved to camp out with an open fire and hunt crawdads with the other boys of the town. Gib's mother was blind and devoted to her son, who spent his time at home helping her with whatever she needed done. But sitting in his seat at school one day, he turned to the girl behind him and said, "If my dad goes to war, I'm going with him."

On November 29, 1861, Lt. Cyrus Elwood of the Home Guard Company attached to Camp Washington came to Clinton County to recruit men for the Union Army. His commander, Col. William Gilmore, had told him to try to enroll men by persuasion but to use threats, even force, if necessary.

Elwood, however, would rather have "real volunteers" than impressed soldiers. As he entered Clinton County at Port Union, the first volunteer to step forward was ten-year-old Gilbert Van Zandt. Gilbert offered to accompany the lieutenant and beat the drum to help him draw a crowd. Nancy Van Zandt had made her little boy a cute army uniform so that he could help Lieutenant Elwood. He followed Elwood from town to town until the lieutenant had enough volunteers to create the Ohio 79th Volunteer Infantry (OVI). Young Gilbert Van Zandt began his career in the Union Army already a hero.

Following the marching beat laid down by this little boy, the men of Clinton and Fayette Counties trooped into Camp Dennison to volunteer. Gilbert's father and cousins were quick to sign up. President Lincoln had called for seventy-five thousand volunteers to put down the rebellion in the South; Ohio answered with thirty thousand men in just ten days.

Mrs. Van Zandt knew her husband and his cousins would volunteer to fight, but she thought Gib would be home in a few days after the recruitment was over. She never guessed that Gib would also volunteer. All she ever said about it was, "Wartime makes folks do funny things. . . ." His father might have stopped him, but when he saw how the officers looked after the boy, he was certain Gib would be okay. Anyway, he would be in Company D with his father.

Military life was mesmerizing to a ten-year-old boy who had not yet seen the horrors of war. The camping, the fireside songs, the drills and marching, and even the rowdiness of the men, all were pretty exciting to a young boy. By the time of the first engagement, Lil' Gib was the unit's official drummer boy.

Gib wrote home often. He wrote about the new friends he was meeting and of the battles he witnessed. He said that the worst part of it all was beating the "Death March" on the drum while they buried his friends. "We had a good many to die; and oh how sad I felt beating the dead march going to their graves. These things I will never forget . . . but I like being a soldier and will see the end of this war if I live. . . ."

Lil' Gib was conspicuous in his bravery under fire. When he captured a Confederate drum at Chattanooga in May 1862, he used it throughout the rest of the war. His company recognized his bravery in the Battle of Nashville by giving him a drum painted gold and silver.

Gib's little legs were so short—he was just a little over four feet tall—that he couldn't keep up with the men on a long march. His captain solved that problem by confiscating a pony for the boy to ride. Gib named the pony Fannie Lee, for a favorite aunt.

After the capture of Nashville, Gen. Ulysses S. Grant took over control of the Union Army. Gib and the Ohio 79th were under the command of Gen. William Tecumseh Sherman. Sherman marched to the sea, burning Atlanta and committing his troops to "total war." He destroyed rail lines and farms in a fifty-mile-wide swathe from Atlanta to Savannah.

During one particularly heated battle, Gen. R. A. Alger called for a messenger to take orders to the front. Gib and Fannie Lee rode up at the ready. Gib looked so small that Alger said, "Send another man." But Gib wouldn't have it. "I can do anything a man can do," he said. Alger handed him the message as he trotted off into the thick of the battle. Late that night, Gib returned and handed the general the receipt proving that the message had been delivered. General Alger promoted him to courier.

As a courier, Gib proved to be swift and dependable. He always took the most direct route to deliver orders, even under withering fire.

Gib came through the war unharmed. When he mustered out with his unit, the 79th OVI marched in review at Washington on June 9, 1865. President Andrew Johnson was there to see the men off. Gilbert rode his pony at the head of the column. Captain Snell introduced Gib, telling the president that "he's a most gentlemanly fellow." He still looked much like a child, but he had proven that he was as good as any man in the Army. Johnson had been informed of Gib's brave service and offered him an appointment to West Point or anything else he might want. After a moment's hesitation, Gilbert said, "I want to keep Fannie Lee and to go home."

"You shall have your wish," said the president.

Despite his glorious service in the Grand Army of the Republic, Gib never spoke about the Civil War. All Lil' Gib wanted was to return home with his horse. The president arranged for Fannie Lee to accompany the 79th on the train for their return trip to Ohio. Back at Port Union, Gib reentered grade school and studied hard. In 1869 his family moved to Xenia, where he finished high school and became a schoolteacher.

Lil' Gib never participated in the parades that honored the men for their service. His younger brother rode Fannie Lee in the Xenia Fourth of July parade in 1870. Gib never sought the spotlight. He had a duty, and he did it.

After his mother died in 1925, one of the last of the Civil War mothers, Gib traveled throughout the West, briefly clerking for Marshall Field's in Chicago. He kept his honorable discharge on the wall in his bedroom until his death.

Gilbert Van Zandt, one of the youngest boys to serve in the Union Army, died in Kansas City, Missouri, on October 4, 1944, at the age of ninety-two.

The Ohio Historical Society placed a bronze memorial marker at his birthplace in Port Union, Ohio.

LITTLE SURE SHOT GETS STARTED

1868

It was early fall of 1868. Nose twitching and tail flicking, a squirrel hopped along a fence top, headed for a hickory nut lodged in a crack. Before he reached it, there was a flash of fire from an old Kentucky rifle; the squirrel dropped to the ground, drilled neatly through the head. The first shot had been fired by a woman who would fire an estimated two million shots in her lifetime, be called "Ohio's most distinguished daughter" by Warren Harding, and become a legend around the world. Annie Oakley had taken her father's gun from above the fireplace and started her epic career.

At the time she was called Phoebe Ann Mosey (some sources say Mozee) and was all of eight years old. In 1855 her family had moved from Pennsylvania to Darke County, Ohio, in the extreme western part of the state, and she was born in a cabin in Woodland, Ohio (now called Willowdale—near present-day North Star), in 1860.

From her earliest years Annie preferred roaming the woods and fields to indoor and more "ladylike" pursuits. Her interest in trapping and hunting turned out to be a blessing, since her father died in 1866 after a trip to the mill in a heavy snowstorm, and the family was in dire straits after that. Her well-timed shots put food on the table and much-needed money in the family till. As she said in her autobiography, "From the time I was ten, I never had a dollar that I did not earn." Even so, she spent several years in the county "poor farm" until she managed to make enough to not only support the family but also pay off her mother's mortgage.

How did she make it? She made a deal with storekeepers in nearby Greenville, Ohio, to sell them all the game she could provide. She shipped rabbits, quail, and ruffed grouse by mail coach to Katzenberger's grocery, and they sold them to hotels and restaurants in Cincinnati. She never shot sitting game, she said, only game on the move, "which gave them a fair chance and made me quick of eye and hand." Her shots were so well placed that diners did not have to munch through buckshot to enjoy a meal.

Annie continued to hone her shooting skills, and by the time she was in her teens, few were willing to face her in the turkey shoots and the like that were one of the main entertainments of the age. In spring 1881, however, came a shooting match that launched this Ohio native into her career as one of the best-known "Western" stars of that or any age.

Crack shooter (and Irish immigrant) Frank Butler was killing time in Cincinnati, waiting to report to a circus engagement he had contracted for in Columbus. Fellow guests in the hotel bet him $100 (the equivalent of about $2,000 then) that he couldn't beat a nearby shooter they knew. "I thought there were some country people who thought they could shoot a little and were willing to lose money, and as I needed it, I went," he recalled.

Frank, twenty-four years old at the time, traveled eighty miles north to Darke County to face this woodland wonder. His opponent turned out to be a twenty-two-year-old woman, who beat him soundly—Annie Mosey.

Frank turned this defeat into a victory of another kind by court-ing Annie, and they married in 1882. She started out by helping him with his act, but he soon realized that her talents overshadowed his and became her manager, an arrangement that benefited them both for a lifetime. He made one thing clear: "I taught her how to do fancy [showmanlike] shooting, but not how to shoot!"

About this time Annie also took the stage name Annie Oakley, some say from the Cincinnati suburb of that name in which the couple lived for a while. In the course of the pair's travels giving shooting shows, Annie met the renowned Sioux chief Sitting Bull in St. Paul, Minnesota. He was so awed by her shooting skills that he gave her a Sioux name that has been translated to "Little Sure Shot."

Later that year, with the help of an advertisement placed by Frank, Annie made an important career move. She joined Buffalo Bill's Wild West Show and Exhibition, which has been called the greatest outdoor show in American history. She was their star for more than six years before she moved on to headline other shows and expositions.

It's easy to understand why. Annie was a petite, attractive woman with long dark hair and an innocent look who came on waving and blowing kisses, wearing a skirt just below her knees, a loose-fitting blouse (to give her freedom of movement), and pearl-buttoned leg-gings. She proceeded to do astonishing things with her shotgun, rifle, and pistol, showing incredible accuracy in feats that included shooting with a gun held upside down above her head as she lay on her back and aimed while looking in a mirror. She could shoot with either hand, and after a target (such as a pigeon) was released, she could run, pick a shotgun off the ground, and hit the bird before it flew away. She could hit playing cards on edge from more than thirty paces, and shoot a cigarette from her husband's mouth or a dime from his hand. In fact, she hit such a high percentage of her targets that she occasionally missed a few on purpose to lend credibility to the show. Her marksmanship won the respect of grizzled American woodsmen and snobby English shooting clubs alike.

No rival ever outshot her, and though the "fancy shooting" scene had plenty of cheaters, she was never one of them. Annie was a crack rider, too, which only added to her "Western" allure.

In more than forty years on the shooting-show circuit, she traveled the country and much of Europe, becoming the darling of England, France, Germany, and other nations as well the United States. She did command performances for princes, prime ministers, and queens and became a legend and an icon. Books, movies, Broadway plays, and eventually TV series were based on her. She won so many awards and citations that if she ever tried to wear all of her medals at once she would probably have collapsed.

Through all of this, Annie stayed simple, modest, practical, and thrifty, sewing her own costumes and never getting caught up in "fame." One of the causes she quietly espoused was the quest of getting women to learn to shoot. Annie might never be willing to wear trousers (she thought that was unfeminine), but she firmly believed that all women should be willing and able to take up arms to defend themselves should the need arise. Cold steel to the cheek should not be an exclusively masculine preserve, so she taught more than fifteen thousand women to shoot in her lifetime.

Though Annie and her husband lived in New Jersey for a while (during an extended engagement of the Wild West show in the Big Apple) and enjoyed staying at Pinehurst, North Carolina, and other places, Ohio remained close to her heart. She and Frank often spent winters on the family farm in Darke County, relaxing and catching up. Frank was once quoted as saying, "A pig in Ohio lives better than a gentleman in New York." And the award Annie treasured most—featured on her posters across the country—was a silver loving cup given to her by "old friends in Greeneville, Ohio."

Annie, whose shooting skills remained undimmed to the end of her life, moved back to Ohio (Dayton) in 1924 and chose the plot in her hometown where she is buried today. A stretch of OH 127 in Darke County is named the Annie Oakley Highway in her honor.

AN INTEMPERATE
TEMPERANCE WOMAN

1880

Even though she was his daughter-in-law, when the tall woman wearing mourning clothes came into his tavern in Sidney, Ohio, Harry Gloyd didn't know quite what to expect. Harry knew that his daughter-in-law Carrie was a teetotaler and that she had watched alcohol kill her husband, so why was she here?

Suddenly Carrie pulled an ax out from under her cloak and swept the drinks off the bar. She stepped behind the bar, crushed all the whiskey bottles, and smashed the beautiful mirrors Harry had brought all the way from Boston. Then she split open the bungs and tops of the beer barrels before she started chopping on the bar itself. The patrons grabbed their whiskey glasses and cowered into one corner of the tavern.

In 1880 a great warrior had arisen to fight the good fight in Ohio and the rest of the country. Carry A. Nation, a name that Carrie Amelia Gloyd Nation had trademarked, lived in Shelby County, Ohio, and had been married to Dr. Charles Gloyd, the "town drunk."

Shortly after Charles's death (Carrie blamed "the curse of drink and alcohol" for it), she began her career as an enemy of alcohol.

Six feet tall and weighing more than 175 pounds, she embarked on a program of "education by hatchetation." She entered taverns throughout Shelby County, shouting prayers for the souls of wicked alcoholics and smashing the bottles and furniture with her ax.

Carrie believed she was the "bulldog running along at the feet of Jesus, barking at what He doesn't like." She called whiskey "a cruel tyrant," and between 1900 and 1910 she was arrested more than thirty times for attacking drinking establishments. Even like-minded individuals thought her actions extreme. Her harangue of the tavern keepers and their patrons, and the damage she inflicted on private property, made her a pariah among Ohio's Anti-Saloon League. All the locals were relieved when she moved to Nebraska.

The temperance movement in Ohio dates back to the 1820s, when Summit County founded the first Temperance Society in the country. The genteel ladies of the society knew that alcohol was the lubricant of labor in Ohio. Many workingmen were paid partially in whiskey. During the construction of Ohio's canal system, ten ounces of whiskey was part of the pay at the end of a long day's labor.

Corn whiskey was an important cash crop in early Ohio, and spirits were served at community events of all kinds. The "town drunk" could expect public censure, but whiskey was integral to social interaction—the tavern was the public meeting place and where citizens got their news. Everyone "knew" whiskey warded off the chill and was a cure for fever and chronic aches and pains. Thus the goal of the Temperance Society wasn't so much to get the men to stop drinking as it was to moderate, or "temper," their alcohol consumption.

This was the Victorian Age, and in 1893 the women of quality in Ohio felt that the urban poor in particular were losing touch with their moral bearing and religious values. The cause of this devastation of lives was "demon rum." Alcohol abuse ruined families, marriages, and the moral fabric of society.

The women of Ohio became particularly active in pursuit of their goal of reducing alcohol consumption. Churchwomen all over Ohio had formed chapters of the Women's Christian Temperance Union (WCTU). They were marching in Washington Court House, Cleveland, and every major city. Eliza Jane Trimble (aka "Mother Thompson") in Hillsboro, a small town that had no fewer than twenty taverns and drugstores that sold liquor, led the WCTU to the taverns downtown, where they knelt and prayed and harassed the bar owners and their customers. It was only the deference of the times that prevented the male tavern keepers and their patrons from pelting the women with beer bottles.

An odd turn of Ohio's constitution gave conservative rural areas control of the state legislature. Periodically the legislature passed laws that they hoped would stifle the use of intoxicants. But the cities were home to many immigrants who used alcohol as one of the few enjoyments of their hard life.

Legislation was a nonviolent approach and not the embarrassment to the temperance movement that Carrie Nation had become. The Ohio Legislature passed the Pond Act, a law that set a tax on the manufacture of liquor, not on sale of liquor itself. Supporters of the act felt that if they raised the price of alcohol, people would buy less and thus consume less. Shortly thereafter, they imposed a sales tax on the purchase of alcohol and prohibited Sunday sales. The liquor interests challenged the laws, and the Ohio Supreme Court ruled that the Pond Act and the Scott Law violated Ohio's constitutional provision against taxing whiskey.

Ohio was the perfect place for the "Battle of the Wets and Drys." The Ohio Anti-Saloon League, formed in Oberlin in 1893, was successful in drawing together the forces of the WCTU and the various chapters of the Temperance Society. Since women had no political power, men are often mentioned as the founders and leaders of the league. Ohio's Howard Hyde Russell is listed as the original founder of the Anti-Saloon League and became its national superintendent.

Politically these two organizations had slightly different goals. The WCTU wanted to moderate alcohol use; the Anti-Saloon League wanted to prohibit it. But together they became a potent political force. Ohio's Rose Law gave "Home Rule" status to the cities, splitting political power between conservative rural areas and the big cities with their immigrant populations. The law permitted Hamilton County to vote to be "dry," closing all the taverns and cutting off the sale of liquor, while Cincinnati remained "wet." The German brewers of Cincinnati and their patrons could make and drink beer, as could the Irish, who preferred whiskey. All the while, the conservative rural folk could impose their morality on their neighbors, barring the sale and consumption of alcohol entirely.

Political office became the political battleground for the Wet and the Dry proponents. The prohibition crowd candidates were called names like "Bone Dry Fry" and "Sun Dried Bill" and were usually Republicans. "Dripping Wet" Bob Buckley, a Democrat, represented Ohio in the U.S. Senate. "Sopping Wet Willie" and "Wringing Wet Ritter" were typical nicknames among the anti-prohibitionists.

Attempts to amend Ohio's constitution to prohibit alcohol manufacture and sales were made in 1914, 1915, and 1917—all were soundly defeated. Only in 1919 did low voter turnout allow the prohibitionists to win, although by a margin of only twenty-six thousand votes. Their win, at least in part, was due to xenophobia and racist tactics. During World War I, prohibitionists used anti-German sentiment against Ohio's brewers, who were mostly German. Anti-Catholic and anti-Irish prejudices also fueled the prohibitionist fires. By 1927 nineteen of Ohio's twenty-two congressmen were "drys."

So very few people in Ohio were surprised when the Eighteenth Amendment made Prohibition the law of the land. What did surprise the "Drys" was how fast the "Wets" bounced back. They passed a resolution to repeal Ohio's ratification of the amendment. When the U.S. Supreme Court ruled against Ohio and disallowed the repeal, the Ohio Legislature moved to punish any judges who heard liquor-related cases. Normally a magistrate was paid a fee for each case he heard, but the legislature passed a law that stripped judges of their fees for hearing a Prohibition case. Obviously the judges didn't waste their time on cases where they wouldn't get paid.

By 1933 the issue was moot. Most of America perceived the "Great Experiment" in legislating social morality to have been a failure. The Twenty-first Amendment to the Constitution repealed Prohibition. Cheers!

OHIO GIVES FLIGHT TO THE WORLD

1900

Building a glider was not particularly difficult. Wilbur had built models that soared hundreds of feet. Surely he could build one that would carry a man. Balloons were already filling the skies, but getting a glider to stay aloft long enough to become a useful means of transportation was a much more challenging proposition. Wilbur visited his cabinetmaking neighbor and learned that he could split wood until he had pieces only a fraction of an inch thick; but when bent, their strength was multiplied.

As a self-trained engineer and inventor, Wilbur saw the possibilities. Properly constructed, a bi-wing glider would be light enough that one man could carry it. He was sure he could convince his younger, lighter brother, Orville, to fly it. The Huffman farm (now a part of Wright-Patterson Air Force Base) near Piqua had a tall barn with a more than sixty-foot drop from the gable to the ground. The barn lot slanted down to a creek, where the field opened up flat for several hundred yards. It was perfect.

Hoisting the glider to the top of the barn was accomplished with pulleys and tackle. For the first test, Wilbur just shoved the glider off the roof and let it soar into the air. It veered to the east and then slowly glided toward the ground in circles. But then, twenty feet from the ground, the right wing dipped and . . . crash. Wilbur calculated that a man, suspended inside the glider, could shift his weight and direct the glider, keeping it aloft. That would be Orville's job.

Orville Wright, born at the family's new home in Dayton, Ohio, on August 19, 1871, was the daring, mischievous one of the two boys. With his brother Wilbur, he opened a bicycle shop on Main Street in Dayton. They were successful because they were always improving their product. Whatever contraption older brother Wilbur could concoct, Orville was willing to ride down a hill or jump off the side of a building with to see how well it worked. Using a bicycle that Wilbur had modified, Orville claimed to have become the Cycling Champion of Ohio.

In the little shop on Main Street where they built, sold, repaired, and readied bikes to race, they even designed a new style bike that sold for $48—a huge sum back then. They made enough money in the shop to allow them to tinker with new inventions. They motorized a bicycle, creating one of the first motorcycles. But Wilbur was enthralled with the idea of a powered manned aircraft. Orville promised his brother that he would fly anything they could put in the air.

After Orville proved he could guide the glider by shifting his weight, pitching the wing enough to steer left or right, the problem of keeping the glider in the air proved more difficult to master. It wasn't enough just to drift left or right. In manned flight, the main problem was controlling the aircraft once it was airborne.

In July 1899, while observing birds in flight, Wilbur determined that a subtle shifting of the glider's wingtips was what was needed to sustain flight—a "system that twisted or warped the wing" like a bird does to take advantage of the lift created by air over the wing. He was sure that he had grasped something profound.

After three years of experimentation, and hundreds of glider crashes, the Wright brothers invented a three-axis controller that allowed a pilot to steer the aircraft while keeping it level and under control. The controls permitted the airplane to roll left or right, pull up or descend, and return to level flight.

After conquering the problem of steering control, the brothers focused on power sources. The drop from the barn roof did not create enough uplift to sustain the weight of a gasoline engine. The brothers created a wind tunnel in their aeronautics laboratory in the rear of the bike shop to test the aerodynamics of their designs—to give the wings more lift, make the propellers and the body of the aircraft sturdier, and make the craft more efficient and safer.

Now they were ready for the real test. The rolling hills of western Ohio did not allow the wind to build up long enough to keep the aircraft in flight. They needed a site with sustained winds. The United States Weather Bureau suggested the sandy plains of coastal North Carolina. To test their 1903 model in real-time flight, they took their aircraft to Kill Devil Hill near Kitty Hawk, North Carolina. There, on a windy hill, they achieved the first manned flight in a heavier-than-air powered craft on December 17, 1903. Their success in getting man into the air eventually propelled men into outer space.

The Wright brothers earned hundreds of flight-related patents in their lifetimes. Wilbur died in 1912 at only forty-five years of age; but Orville, who passed away in 1948, lived to see jet aircraft. After having taken man into the air, Orville lived to see an aircraft fly at more than one thousand miles an hour.

Powered flight gave birth to a whole new industry, and Ohio became home to many of its inventions. Aircraft-related industries arose in

Dayton, Akron, Niles, Alliance, Sandusky, Cleveland, and Cincin-nati. By 1910 freight was being hauled from Dayton to Columbus by airplane. A crop-dusting industry began in Troy, Ohio, around 1921; and Dayton was seeding clouds to increase rainfall by 1923.

Wright State University in Dayton was named in honor of the brothers. And when James M. Cox became Ohio's governor, he built one of the first municipal airports in the country (in 1928) between Dayton and Vandalia. Near the entranceway of Cox International Airport is a full-size replica of the first Wright bi-wing "Flyer."

When World War I broke out, Ohio's experience in flight was put to good use. The Goodyear Rubber Company plant in Akron began producing lighter-than-air craft (dirigibles) for hauling heavy freight and to use as battlefield observation posts.

But it wasn't just the Wright brothers who led Ohio to put the legend "Birthplace of Aviation" on their license plates. A racecar driver named Eddie Rickenbacker became America's greatest fighter pilot during World War I. Rickenbacker was a driver for U.S. Army officers until he met Col. Billy Mitchell. Mitchell was lobbying the Army to build an air corps and believed that he could change the course of the war with airpower. Rickenbacker convinced Mitchell that he was the man to bring air power to the Army. In the course of the war, Rickenbacker flew hundreds of flights over enemy territory, bombing and strafing enemy targets. He shot down so many German aircraft that he became known as the "Ace of Aces." For these feats of derring-do, he became the first airman to earn the Congressional Medal of Honor.

On February 2, 1962, Ohio's air supremacy was cemented forever. Col. John Glenn piloted the first spacecraft (Friendship 7) to circumnavigate the earth. In four hours, fifty-five minutes, and twenty-three seconds, traveling at 17,500 miles an hour, Glenn became the first man to circle the world in space. Toward the end of a long and honorable career (1974–99) in the U.S. Senate, in 1998 Glenn became the oldest person to make a space flight. He joined the crew of the space shuttle *Discovery* on a nine-day mission. Traveling more than 3.6 million miles, he performed experiments and participated in a study of the effects of extended space travel on human aging.

In 1966 Neil Armstrong of Wapakoneta, Ohio, was the command pilot of *Gemini 8.* Three years later he became the first person to step onto the face of the moon with "one small step for man; one giant leap for mankind." Both Glenn and Armstrong were awarded the Congressional Space Medal of Honor.

Twenty-one other Ohioans, men and women, have served the nation in the corps of astronauts. Judith Resnick, an engineer from Akron, was on the space shuttle *Challenger* when it exploded shortly after liftoff on January 28, 1986.

The Neil Armstrong Air and Space Museum at Wapakoneta and the NASA Glenn Visitor Center in Cleveland are major tourist destinations for Ohio's space buffs and visitors. The National Museum of the U.S. Air Force at Wright-Patterson Air Force Base just east of Dayton contains the largest collection of historical aircraft in the world. Planes on display can be seen and often entered by the public, free of charge. Current exhibits run the gamut from the Wright brothers to the B1 bomber. In Cleveland the International Women's Air and Space Museum honors women in flight. All told, visitors can explore eighteen air and space museums in Ohio.

THE CON WOMAN OF
MILLIONAIRES' ROW

1904

Everyone was shocked in November 1904 when Cassie Chadwick was arrested while still wearing her money belt containing more than $100,000. Cassie was a fraud who had conned the banks and her rich "friends" out of millions.

Right up to that point, Cassie L. Chadwick was the "Queen of Ohio" and the belle of the ball at every soiree given in Cleveland. Everyone believed she was the illegitimate daughter of Andrew Carnegie, but that didn't matter since she was the obvious heir to his millions, or at least the $400 million she said he had promised her. She claimed that Carnegie was so racked with guilt that he showered her with gifts and money, with which she maintained an opulent lifestyle. Everyone was curious about her and sought her company.

Chadwick Mansion on Euclid Avenue was a favorite haunt of the rich and famous. Cleveland's Euclid Avenue was unparalleled in its beauty and the wealth of its inhabitants. Majestic elm trees lined both sides of the street, and there was a broad, parklike strip down the middle of the road. Homes on both sides of the street were mansions that could only be described as the most fabulous in America. At its height, the real estate tax valuation of the mansions along Euclid Avenue was higher than the assessment of Fifth Avenue in New York City. *Baedeker's Travel Guide* called Millionaires' Row "the Showplace of America."

Millionaires' Row was never more illustrious than when resident John Davison Rockefeller (1839–1937) became the world's richest man and America's first billionaire. He founded the Standard Oil Company in 1870 and used his money and power to structure a monopoly that controlled every aspect of the oil delivery system. In 1911 the U.S. Supreme Court found his business practices to be an illegal restraint of trade, but in the meantime he amassed a fortune unsurpassed in his time.

In 1859 Rockefeller drilled his first oil well and built a refinery in Cleveland. His keen eye for a bargain soon put him in a position to take advantage of the economic boom that followed the Civil War. By undercutting his competitors in what came to be called the "Cleveland Conquest," he acquired control of 90 percent of the oil in the United States.

Rockefeller felt that intense competition was bad for business. He controlled the drilling, refining, transporting, marketing, and end sale of his products. His business practices were brutal, and he used his wealth as a weapon to bankrupt the competition. Newspapers called his company "the most cruel, impudent, pitiless, and grasping monopoly that ever fastened upon a country."

Rockefeller's neighbor on Millionaires' Row was Alfred Atmore Pope (1842–1913). A steel manufacturer, he became a patron of the arts. He purchased works by Manet, Monet, Degas, Pissaro, and Renoir and supported American artists Mary Cassatt and James

Whistler. Today many of the works are on permanent loan to Cleveland art museums.

Euclid Avenue's fabulously wealthy men dabbled in politics, but none of them succeeded the way Marcus Alonzo Hanna (1837–1904) did. Hanna is well known for having said, "There are two things that are important in politics. The first is money, and I can't remember the second." With Hanna's money, William McKinley never needed to leave his front porch to make a political speech on the road to the White House.

Hanna deplored that "damned cowboy" Teddy Roosevelt. But when McKinley ran for reelection, Roosevelt was on the ticket. Hanna exclaimed, "Don't any of you realize there's only one life between that madman and the presidency?" Yet after McKinley's assassination, Hanna helped Roosevelt secure the Panama Canal.

Another millionaire on Euclid was Charles Francis Brush (1849–1929), who began experimenting with electricity before he was twelve years old. He designed a new type of electric "dynamo" and the arc lights that made Cleveland the first city in America to have electric streetlights and brightened city streets across the country.

Brush used his Millionaires' Row mansion to showcase his newest inventions. He harnessed wind power to generate electricity for his own home. During the worst storms, the Brush mansion was never without power. Today the principles of Brush's wind-powered generators are being adapted to create "green" energy.

The Chadwicks lived just down the block. Cassie Chadwick was born Elizabeth Bigley in 1857 in Canada. A liar and dreamer, she opened a checking account at age thirteen on which she drew several worthless checks. Arrested for forgery, she was released as a juvenile. The court thought she was insane.

She moved to Cleveland to live with her sister Alice. Soon she had her own apartment. Claiming to be a widow and going by the name Madame Lydia DeVere, she began operating as a psychic and clairvoyant. In 1882 Lydia married Dr. Wallace Springsteen. When her wedding picture appeared in the local papers, her creditors started calling, demanding to be paid. Springsteen threw her out. Changing her name to Madame Marie LaRose, she reestablished her fortune-telling business and sought husband number two.

Soon she married a well-to-do farmer named John Scott, whom she convinced to sign a prenuptial agreement that provided for her should the marriage fail. She shortly filed for divorce, claiming that Scott had committed adultery. Her divorce settlement became the seed money for her next venture.

In the 1890 census she identified herself as a childless widow. In truth, she had a four-year-old son, Emil. By that time she was calling herself Mrs. Cassie Hoover. She opened a brothel, where she met husband number three, Dr. Leroy Chadwick. Cassie represented herself as a respectable widow operating a boarding-house. When Dr. Chadwick informed her that her place was a well-known whorehouse, she "fainted." Cassie claimed to know nothing about that profession and begged the good doctor to take her away lest people think she was part of it. Young Emil Hoover was left in the care of the girls at the brothel as Cassie married Dr. Chadwick in 1897.

That same year she began her career as the illegitimate daughter of Andrew Carnegie. She convinced a New York lawyer that she was Carnegie's daughter, claiming he had given her $7 million in promissory notes and that on his death she would receive another $400 million. Lawyer Dillon arranged for her to keep the forged documents in a safe deposit box. She had guessed correctly that no one was brave enough to ask the wealthy Carnegie if he had an illegitimate daughter. Using the forged documents as collateral, she borrowed millions.

In November 1904 a Boston banker demanded repayment of a $190,000 loan. When Mrs. Chadwick couldn't cover the note, the bank sued. Soon all her fraudulent loans came due, more than $5 million. When the banks turned to Carnegie for payment, he denied ever knowing her.

Shock waves shot through the Cleveland banking district, and some banks were forced into receivership. Cassie's neighbors on Millionaires' Row crowded into court in disbelief. Even Andrew Carnegie came, unable to believe that such a monstrous fraud could have been perpetrated in his name. The morning of the trial, Leroy Chadwick and his daughter boarded a steamer for Europe—just hours after his attorney served Cassie with divorce papers.

Cassie L. Chadwick was found guilty of seven counts of forgery and conspiracy. She died on her birthday in 1907 at the Ohio State Penitentiary, in a cell not nearly as fine as Millionaires' Row.

The Lake View Cemetery at the other end of Euclid Avenue is the final resting place of many of the inhabitants of Millionaires' Row. Graves and mausoleums of the rich and famous are tourist attractions. Visit the Lake View Cemetery's Web site for the final resting place of the illuminati.

THE DROWNING OF DAYTON

1913

In retrospect, it might possibly have been prevented. When the earliest settlers, led by one Israel Ludlow, laid out the beginnings of this southwestern Ohio city in 1796, they chose a spot not merely near a river, as settlers were wont to do, but in a low-lying area right at the confluence of four of them. The fifty or so log cabins and frame houses that formed the nucleus of Dayton—despite many warnings from local Native Americans about floods—were set right where the Great Miami River is joined by its major tributaries, the Mad and Stillwater rivers, and Wolf Creek.

The settlement did suffer floods from time to time, so the inhabitants eventually built levees to try and protect themselves. After a particularly bad flood in 1898, they were actually planning to make more serious provisions to address this problem. But nature delivered a big surprise in the very month, March 1913, when they intended to start in on this project.

On March 23, Easter Sunday, two big storms arrived so close on each other's heels that they were indistinguishable, dumping heavy rain over much of the entire state for three days straight. Never before in recorded history had so much rain (in some places more than ten inches) ever fallen in Ohio within such a short time.

The ground was already saturated and rivers everywhere close to flood stage. The floods that soon followed affected more than one hundred Ohio towns and cities, eventually causing at least 467 deaths across the state and nearly $300 million worth of property damage. This flooding did more damage in a single day than all the Indian wars in Ohio history, and this event is often called "Ohio's greatest natural disaster."

The hardest hit of all was Dayton. On March 25 the rivers around Dayton crested, and as the *Ohio Almanac* puts it, "The city was deluged with 1.5 million gallons of water per second, an incredible torrent that equaled an entire month's flow over Niagara Falls." As the water poured over the levees, the downtown of Dayton, which sits right on the riverside, was soon twenty feet deep in muddy water. By the evening of this day, fourteen square miles of Dayton were inundated.

As the flood climbed toward the second stories of buildings, power was cut off; fires and explosions followed in the wake of broken gas mains. As the fast-flowing water moved through the streets, it knocked down light poles, washed out bridges, smashed store windows, and carried wreckage along with it to inflict further damages elsewhere. Everywhere citizens climbed to rooftops and attics to escape the rising waters. More than 1,500 horses and other animals drowned along with the more than 360 people unfortunate enough to be caught directly in the deluge. At least twenty thousand homes and many businesses were destroyed, and countless homes and trees were uprooted and washed away. Nurses rushed to carry patients to the upper floors of hospitals, and 45,000 books were damaged beyond repair as water swept into the city library.

As the city government of Dayton groped for ways to deal with the disaster, an amazing private citizen stepped into the vacuum. John Patterson, the head of the National Cash Register Company, Dayton's largest employer, had already shown himself to be an enlightened, effective, and groundbreaking businessman. NCR was not only very profitable but also one of the first companies ever to have a Human Resources department, a campus-style industrial park, and amenities like showers and exercise facilities for workers.

The governor of Ohio appointed Patterson head of the Dayton Relief Committee, and he quickly took control of the rescue efforts. He turned his giant factory into a shelter and relief center and set his entire workforce of more than seven thousand to work on rescue operations. His buildings and employees fed the hungry, housed the homeless, treated those in need of medical attention, communicated with the horrified Americans across the country who were anxious about the fate of Dayton, and built wooden boats to help rescue those marooned on roofs, trees, and upper stories.

The formidable forces of NCR were joined later by the Red Cross and the Ohio National Guard, the latter maintaining order and erecting tent cities to help house the displaced. Donations from around the country also arrived—even from hard-hearted New York City—to help with rescue and rehabilitation.

By Friday of this dark week, March 25, the floodwaters receded and the last marooned citizens were able to descend from their perches to return to their homes, if they still stood, to assess the damage. The cleanup and rebuilding of Dayton took more than a year, and total economic recovery took much longer. But there was one improvement for which the citizens were not going to wait. As Walter Havighurst noted, "Three weeks after the flood, crowds gathered at the water-stained courthouse with a sign: remember the promises you made in the attic!" Within a very short time, private citizens had ponied up more than $2 million for a study to figure out how to prevent this horror from ever happening again.

The study was performed by hydrological engineer Arthur Morgan of Minnesota with the aid of fifty more engineers he hired to help assess the entire area and its rainfall, landforms, geology, and runoff patterns. From the array of alternatives Morgan subsequently recommended, Dayton officials chose one that would involve some rechanneling of the river and six earthen dams on the watercourses above the city, plus concrete outlets and spillways. These dams would not hold water at all times—only when the need for impoundment arose.

The cost of this undertaking would be almost $40 million. This price tag, plus opposition from landowners aghast at the idea of taxes to help fund the project and fearful that eminent domain would be invoked and their homes or businesses demolished to build these dams "for the public good," delayed the final legal nod until 1915.

The entire system, officially christened the Miami Conservancy—the first major watershed district in the United States—was completed in 1922. And it has done more than protect the city of Dayton from any floods since, including the serious floods of 1937. The project was a model to the nation and the world for flood control and helped inspire the ambitious Tennessee Valley Authority of the New Deal, which resulted in dams and flood-control measures in seven states of the Southeast.

In more recent years the Miami Conservancy has also helped raise the quality of life in the Dayton area by its studies of water quality and pollution and its River Corridor program, which works to convert riversides to greenbelts and sites for outdoor recreation and entertainment.

OHIO'S ONION FIELD WAR

1934

Hardin County, Ohio, was dominated by picturesque Scioto Marsh. When farmers entered the marshlands in the 1860s, they knew all they had to do to make their fortune was drain the marsh and plant suitable crops. The flat land with its moist, rich soil proved to be perfect for potatoes, carrots, tomatoes, and onions, and twenty-one thousand acres of wet, boggy marsh were soon converted into some of the most productive agricultural land in the nation. By 1880 the Scioto Marsh and the nearby town of McGuffey had become the Onion Capital of the World—and eventually the site of the Hardin County Onion Field War.

By 1934 two-thirds of the area was controlled by twenty-five growers. Another 30 percent was owned by three huge farms. These few growers dictated the wages of the workers who planted, weeded, and harvested the crop. Pickers and weeders worked ten-hour days with only fifteen minutes for lunch. There were no breaks, no restroom facilities, no available sources of drinking water, and no medical aid services. But this was the Great Depression, and 37 percent of

Ohio's workers were unemployed. The growers were paying 12 cents per hour and on some days, only 8 cents. Occasionally the workers were allowed to milk a local cow and take a little produce from the fields to stave off starvation.

Worse, farm labor was seasonal. The onion field workers could only count on a couple months' work. Even so, there was competition for the jobs. The laborers lived in extreme poverty. Farm shanties provided what shelter there was, often twenty or more people to a twenty- by thirty-foot room.

As the Depression worsened, farmers did less to rejuvenate the fields. They spent less on fertilizer and land management. They cut down the willows and poplars at the edges of the fields that helped prevent erosion and sold them for firewood. Crop yields fell every year, and farmers complained of high wages and low productivity. They reduced the amount of acreage under cultivation and laid off laborers. Those who remained worked stooped over in fields where the temperature of the black soil could reach 120 degrees.

Ohio had a long history of unionization. In good times, a number of industries had found it useful to bargain with workers to retain good people. But the growers in the 1930s knew that there were a dozen men looking for work for every job that was available. And they knew that those men would take whatever the growers were willing to pay.

In defense of their families and their right to work, the onion field laborers voted to form a union. On June 18 and 19, 1934, the American Federation of Labor recognized Union Local 19724, the Agricultural Workers Union (AWU), the first nationally recognized agricultural union. Its leader was Okey Odell.

J. M. Rizor of the International Quarrymen's Union came to Hardin County to help organize the new union. Rizor helped the agricultural workers develop their demands for better working conditions. Theirs was exhausting, backbreaking labor. They wanted periodic rest breaks, toilet facilities, an eight-hour workday, and 35 cents an hour.

Workers in town were paid more than that. They were allowed reasonable breaks; they had toilets and in some cases, shower and medical facilities. Farm laborers wanted to be treated with equal dignity.

The growers organized to oppose the union. They formed the Onion Grower's Association, which refused to meet with the farm labor union. They claimed they couldn't make a profit as things were and would "let the fields grow over with weeds" rather than meet the workers' demands.

The AWU pointed out the obvious prosperity of many of the growers and demanded to see the growers' account books. The growers refused. The Ohio Legislature then asked the growers for an independent audit to determine if they could pay the wages requested; the growers again refused.

With the growers showing no willingness to negotiate, Odell called for a strike on June 20, 1934. Eight hundred of the workers walked out of the fields. Growers immediately hired replacement workers from among the hundreds of unemployed men in the surrounding communities. The union members took up posts to picket the growers' fields.

With the help of the Ohio Unemployed League and the Socialist Party of America, Odell's union members searched vehicles coming into the county to prevent replacement workers (called "scabs") from taking their jobs. They spread nails and debris on the roads into the fields and stoned strikebreakers. Both the Socialist Party and the American Civil Liberties Union (ACLU) raised money for a legal defense fund for union members who were arrested, but their support brought the union under attack for having "communist" sympathies.

Common Pleas Judge Hamilton Hoge issued an injunction restricting the union pickets. The county sheriff hired "special deputies" (paid by the growers) armed with machine guns, grenades, and "mob control" tear gas weapons to police the picketers. These young deputies had been members of the Ohio National Guard, although most were barely over eighteen years of age. In previous strikes in Ohio, the authorities had little compunction about using the National Guard to assist employers in breaking a strike. Governor George White, a Democrat, had no reservations either.

The poorly trained special deputies soon became unruly and began to harass other locals as well as the workers. The sheriff made his own interpretation of Judge Hoge's order to continually arrest picketers for "mob actions." He forced the pickets to stay twenty-five feet apart, then fifty yards, then one hundred yards. On several occasions he called the picketers together, then arrested them for unlawful assembly.

Near the end of June, the U.S. Department of Labor sent negotiators to try to end the strike. When the union rejected the half measures offered by the growers, the growers stepped up their violent attacks on union leaders. Special deputies clubbed the picketers and shot two of the workers.

Strikers fought back with bricks, bottles, and rocks. Wherever strikers and scabs met, fistfights broke out. "Someone" blew up bridges and fired weapons at the scabs. Growers' warehouses were burned, and numerous small explosions erupted in the onion-processing stations.

Odell was walking alone in the city of McGuffey one day when the town marshal arrested him for "congregating." He served ten days in jail with another union organizer. Sixty picketers were also arrested and charged with inciting a riot, malicious destruction of property, and unlawful assembly, but no one was ever brought to trial or convicted.

When the home of McGuffey's mayor was bombed (no one was hurt), the sheriff immediately arrested Odell. He didn't charge Odell, but after a mob of two hundred vigilantes encircled the jail, the sheriff released Odell into the crowd. With the sheriff and fifteen deputies standing on the jailhouse steps, the mob kidnapped Odell and carted him off to a small town twelve miles away, where he was repeatedly beaten and threatened and then left for dead on the side of the road.

The vigilantes returned to McGuffey, where they seized control of the streets and attacked known union members. Ordinary citizens who had nothing to do with the strike were stopped on the street and asked which side they supported. Those who expressed any sympathy for the strikers, and even those who professed to be neutral, were severely beaten. The citizens of McGuffey cowered in their homes.

Odell returned home, only to be met again by the vigilantes. He armed himself and told them to "Go to hell" when they demanded he leave town.

In an attempt to end the violence, Secretary of Labor Francis Perkins (originally from Ohio) sent another federal negotiator. On August 28, 1934, the representative left Hardin County after negotiating a minimum wage of 25 cents per hour. The strike was over. Most of the eight hundred union members had left the county by this time, intimidated by the vigilantes. The growers hired as many replacement workers as they could find, and by the first of September, the onion harvest was well under way.

The small growers acceded to the demands of the union and signed a contract with the remaining union members at the 35 cents per hour Odell had originally requested. Within a few years, the Hardin County growers ceased to hire local workers and began importing Mexican farm labor. Onion production continued to fall as the soil became increasingly depleted. By the mid-1940s the major onion production in the country had relocated to Colorado and Georgia.

Ironically, although the federal government intervened to end Ohio's Onion Field War in 1934, the National Labor Relations Act of 1935 exempted agricultural workers from the protections of the law. As a result, growers were free to coerce and discriminate against farm workers who wished to unionize.

THE NADIR OF ELLIOTT NESS

1938

It was a strange, nightmarish setting in the very midst of the industrial wasteland at the heart of Cleveland's inner city. An area that was once part of a prosperous, thriving manufacturing hub well served by a network of rail lines had, in the wake of the Great Depression and the mass unemployment that followed, become a huge shantytown. Its collection of miserable sheds and shelters made of pieces of scrap tin, scrounged old lumber, and even cardboard was home to a small army of the unemployed, the underemployed, transients ("hoboes," in the parlance of the time), and other unfortunates.

At the edge of this grim expanse, which included the areas the natives called Kingsbury Run and "the Flats," stood a figure of national renown—Elliott Ness, leader of the bribe-proof "Untouchables," the man who helped bring down Al Capone in Chicago. In 1934 he'd been appointed safety director of Cleveland, then considered the most dangerous city in the country, to help lower the crime rate and clear up corruption. Now, four years later, in the wee hours of the morning of August 18, an ax handle over his shoulder, he was leading twenty-five policemen in a swift and relentless surprise attack on, of all things, a hobo jungle.

After all possible escape routes for the inhabitants had been blocked off, and with a fire truck parked nearby to light the scene, the police went from shanty to shanty, loudly rousing the "house-holders," awake or asleep, drunk or sober, and herding them off to the city workhouse. The air filled with curses, complaints, and shrieks (plus the crashes of bashed-in doors). After everyone had been cleared from the settlement (even the men's pets, which were rounded up and packed off by the Animal Protective League), coal oil was spread about and the whole area was torched. Whatever was left of the men's humble possessions after the quick round of scav-enging that preceded the fire was destroyed in the blaze.

What provoked this high-handed invasion, which netted only a few minor criminals and destroyed the only home the inhabitants had?

It was the infamous Torso Killer of Cleveland, and Ness was in charge of the effort to apprehend the murderer. From 1934 to 1938 he, or she, had killed at least a dozen people (there was, and still is, lively disagreement as to exactly how many victims should be attributed to this particular monster's scorecard). And they were not just killed, but killed in a notably awful way—it would have kept the modern-day supermarket "rags" in headlines for years. As one news-paper of the time put it, "Magazines appealing to morbid tastes can-not devise fiction more gruesome than the hard facts of Cleveland's series of torso murders."

After killing his victims (no one is sure where or how), the Torso Murderer decapitated them, emasculated them (when they were men), or cut them into pieces that were then playfully distributed around and near the city to be discovered by horrified citizens. Body parts and pieces were found on the banks and in the waters of Lake Erie and the Cuyahoga River, in trash-filled gullies and ponds, under bridges, in dumps, and in burlap bags, tomato baskets, and plain brown paper wrappers.

Each time a new victim was discovered, there was a massive search for not just the perpetrator but also the rest of the body parts—the latter, often in vain. One high school history teacher later in the century dramatized this for his class with the following little ditty: "Floating down the river, chunk by chunk by chunk, arms and legs and torsos, hunk by hunk by hunk." Even into the 1950s, some Cleveland parents scared their children into behaving with the prospect of this ghoulish phantom.

Only two of the victims were ever clearly identified—and then only because they had police records. The fact that none of these people were ever reported missing by anyone led authorities to conclude that, like the victims of Jack the Ripper in late-nineteenth-century London, the victims were all from the underbelly of society—vagrants, prostitutes, petty lawbreakers, and "bums."

Not that, at least initially, this kept the hunt for the murderer from becoming the most massive search in the history of the Cleveland police department. During the three years within which the Cleveland murders occurred—some people feel that somewhat similar crimes in Youngstown and Pennsylvania were actually related—no stone was left unturned. Not just the regular police but a special task force of detectives, led by renowned supersleuth Peter Merylo (complete with Dick Tracy–style hat), combed every neighborhood near any of the crimes, interviewed everyone imaginable, and followed every possible clue or lead, no matter how tiny. It's been estimated that at least 7,300 people were interrogated, including (since the police theorized that the murderer might be insane) an incredibly rich assortment of oddballs, deviants, and weirdos.

Police sifted through slums, funeral homes, cemeteries, slaughterhouses, abandoned breweries, boxcars, and speakeasies. After rewards were offered, the police received at least fifty tips a day—phone calls and letters. All of this was followed up—to no avail. There was not a single piece of hard evidence. Hence the pent-up frustration that led to Ness's raid on Kingsbury Run in the summer of 1938. If the killer couldn't be caught, maybe he could be deprived of his prey. Or (since all of the unfortunates snatched up that night were fingerprinted) at least if further murders occurred, the victims would be identifiable.

In fairness, the detectives were working at a disadvantage. The science of forensics was in its infancy, and many of the tests now used to identify or trap criminals were not yet devised. Crime scenes were not strictly controlled as they are now, so every time a new discovery was made, scores of people showed up to trample and confuse the scene—and any possible evidence. Plus the police were following the old formula for finding a murderer—first look to those closest to the victim, those most likely to commit a crime of passion. The term "serial murderer" would not be coined until forty years later, by the FBI, to describe a type of killer who might not know his or her victims at all but simply select them at random, or according to some inner template, to fulfill some perverse purpose.

Even without the aid of modern "profiling" and the like, the investigators did eventually reach some fairly sound conclusions: The murderer was a large, strong person; someone very familiar with anatomy (the cuts were very skillfully made); and probably lived near the target area.

With the aid of hindsight and information that has only come to light in recent years, including revelations Ness made to his biographer before he died, one suspect stands out of the many people investigated. Francis Sweeney was a medical doctor who had much experience with amputations during his military service in World War I. He was a big, powerful man as well as an alcoholic, drug abuser, and possibly a schizophrenic—and he lived near Kingsbury

Run. During the investigations he was secretly held in a hotel room for a week by Ness and others, including an expert who administered lie detector tests after the doctor was dried out, which the doctor thoroughly failed.

One week after the raid on Kingsbury Run, Sweeney committed himself to the Sandusky Soldiers and Sailors Home, and the murders stopped. Ness probably thought Sweeney was the culprit, but he had no clear evidence, and the doctor was related to a powerful political opponent of Ness's.

Ness failed to finger the Torso Murderer, and although his other accomplishments in Cleveland were outstanding, this dimmed his law enforcement halo enough that he has been called the murderer's thirteenth victim. To add insult to injury, for years after Ness left Cleveland, he received taunting cards and letters from Dr. Sweeney.

The Police Historical Society in Cleveland has a speculation-provoking collection of death masks of many of the victims, and much more, should you wish to try your own hand at a definitive solution to the mystery.

A STORYBOOK SETTING
COMES TO LIFE

1945

In the 1940s the most famous farm in the world was in Richland County, Ohio, and bore the rather exotic title of Malabar. The fact that it was named for a hill overlooking the harbor in Bombay (now Mumbai), India, should be a hint that this was no ordinary farm.

Malabar was created from four older farms—all with misused and depleted soil—by a man who was determined to prove that there was a better way to treat the land upon which our lives depend. He then worked to return the soil, much of which at that point was "a mixture of cement and gravel with traces of acid," to its original richness by largely natural or organic means, and the farm became a national and worldwide model for sustainable agriculture.

The man was Louis Bromfield—and he managed to write his way into the position to do all of this. Although his grandfather and father had been farmers, Louis became a journalist early on and then a more "serious" writer, becoming rich through writing. His first five novels brought him critical acclaim, including a Pulitzer Prize, as well as making him a millionaire.

When the urge to settle down finally hit him, Louis left France (right before World War II) and bought a farm "overlooking the valley I loved as a boy and still love better than any valley in the world."

On his farm—in addition to those many steadily improving acres of soil—there were stands of timber, spring-fed ponds, and all the sounds, sights, and scents of the country that many city dwellers fantasize about and yearn for. The farm also held a giant barn, outbuildings of all kinds, and a thirty-two-room house that Louis worked with an architect to build, furnished with tastefully chosen antiques, and carefully designed to incorporate all the best of Ohio Country architecture.

All this made for nothing less than a storybook setting, and the prince and princess to fill it were not far behind.

Louis had written a number of screenplays, some for movies made from his own books. During his time in Hollywood, he made many friends whose names appeared on movie theater marquees. Thus, among Malabar's steady stream of visitors and guests were not just artists, other writers, socialites, and fellow farmers but also folks like James Cagney, Errol Flynn, Tyrone Power, Shirley Temple, Dorothy Lamour, Kay Francis, Carole Lombard, and Fay Wray. At any given time, one might find such notables carrying pails of milk, selling veggies at the farm's highly successful farm stand, stirring apple butter, canning tomatoes, running off to buy seed, or helping birth calves as they enthusiastically immersed themselves in the rural life.

One of Louis's closest friends from the West Coast was Humphrey Bogart, the man who in 1997 was voted the Number One Movie Legend of All Time by *Entertainment Weekly* and the Greatest Male Star of All Time in 1999 by the American Film Institute. In

1945 Bogie's life was in greater turmoil than usual. He was forty-five, and his third marriage was so stormy that the press called the couple the Battling Bogarts. And now he'd fallen hard for someone new— his twenty-year-old costar in the film *To Have and Have Not* (her first picture), Lauren Bacall. This was no mere flirtation or one-night stand. Bogie and the slim blonde, nicknamed "the Look," a young woman that Warner Bros. Studio was working hard to turn into their latest sex goddess, were in love. In fact, they hoped to get married. Bromfield thought Malabar would be the perfect place for the quiet wedding the couple wanted the minute Bogart was free to remarry.

The starry-eyed couple agreed, and eleven days after his Reno divorce was finalized, Bogart and Bacall were on the Super Chief headed for Ohio. The most sensational event Richland County ever hosted needed to be accomplished within a rather tight time frame, since the couple had to be back at their studios making pictures in just three days. They arrived at Malabar on Sunday and had one day to relax amidst the frantic preparations for the festivities. The bride-to-be, curlers hidden by a scarf, got the marriage license at the county courthouse the next morning, citing herself as a resident of Lucas, Ohio—after all, she'd spent the whole day and night before there. The required blood tests were given super-quick service by a helpful local doctor.

That thirty-two-room house—the "Big House"—was cleaned, shined, and polished from top to bottom for the event and decorated with flowers and ferns from the farm. The weather on the big day— May 21, 1945—kindly provided a bright blue sky. The wedding was to be held in the high-ceilinged entrance hall, and a select few guests waited there anxiously, including the mother of the bride, who was the matron of honor; Louis Bromfield's mother; his daughter, poised at the piano to play the "Wedding March"; the family cook; and, in honor of the solemnity of the occasion, only one of the Bromfields' many boxer dogs. The hordes of reporters and media photographers were all outside, held at bay by the local police.

When the time came for Lauren to descend the large curving staircase in her new pale-pink woolen suit, she was nowhere to be found. "Where is she?" whispered Bogart nervously. "Hold it, she's in the can!" said the man standing by to hold her arm as she walked down the stairs—not her father, but Louis's longtime secretary and editor, George Hawkins. When Lauren finally emerged from the powder room, she was shaking so hard, orchid bouquet and all, that she wasn't sure she'd make it.

The ceremony itself was short and simple—just three minutes long. Judge Herbert Schettler made it all official, substituting, at the couple's request, the word "cherish" for the word "obey" in the time-honored words of the joining. When Lauren looked over at Bogart, America's all-time tough guy had tears streaming down his cheeks as he said, "I do." "I never realized before what those words really meant—what they should mean," he told her later.

A lucky *Life* magazine photographer was let in after the ceremony to snap the cake-cutting, and eventually the whole pacing herd of media people had a chance to immortalize the event. (Even today, more than sixty years later, you can see a live snippet of the famous wedding at Malabar on YouTube.)

Bromfield gave the couple a boxer puppy and an acre of Malabar for a wedding present. They never got around to building a cottage on that acre, but they did manage that Hollywood miracle—a happy marriage—until Bogart's death twelve years later finally parted them. It helped that Bacall sidelined her own career, by choice, to devote herself to their union.

Malabar had a happy ending too. Bromfield's family deeded the farm to the state in 1972 after his death, and a deal was worked out so that its outstanding debts—his later books did not do as well as his earlier ones—were paid or forgiven. In 1976 Malabar Farm, still a working farm, became a state park and one of north-central Ohio's most popular attractions, hosting 350,000 or more visitors a year.

People still come to Malabar for the sights, sounds, and smells of country living; to see the beef cattle, chickens, and goats and the petting zoo; the fields of corn, wheat, and oats; and the many special events such as spring plowing, maple syrup days, and square dances. They also come to see that big staircase and entranceway where Bogie and Bacall tied the knot, as well as the honeymoon guest room— twin beds, oversize bathtub, ceramic chickens, and all.

PUTTING A MATCH TO PREJUDICE

1954

During a violent thunderstorm in the early morning hours of July 5, 1954, a tall, thin figure darted up to an old two-story schoolhouse on a back street in Hillsboro, Ohio. The person broke the padlock on the door, grabbed two large cans of what would today be called "accelerant" (gas and oil) from the cellar, and splashed their contents over the walls and floor of a classroom upstairs. A lit match quickly followed, and the eighty-five-year-old Lincoln Schoolhouse—the grade school for the town's black children—was ablaze.

The fire department managed to put out the fire before the entire school was destroyed. The blacks living nearby were thoroughly questioned and investigated. When that turned up no suspects, people wondered if maybe the thunderstorm was responsible.

Imagine the astonishment at the next meeting of the city council, July 6, when the county engineer—a well-respected thirty-four-year-old white professional—took the police chief aside and freely admitted that he had set the fire.

The engineer, Phillip Partridge, was a devout Christian and humanitarian. The historic U.S. Supreme Court decision *Brown v. Board of Education* had recently been made, making it clear that the concept of "separate but equal" facilities had no place in American education. But in Hillsboro separate was not exactly equal, since the Lincoln School was inferior in many ways to the white schools in the town. Partridge feared (rightly, as it turned out) that segregation would not disappear swiftly, despite the Court's ruling.

He decided to force the issue by destroying the town's ability to segregate the schoolchildren. He'd been thinking about it for years, he said, as the question of what he could do to help end segregation kept running through his head. He asked the Lord to "show him a way to right the wrongs" being done to blacks in the area, and then he went one step further and asked for a divine wake-up call to help him achieve his mission. The Lord—or the lightning—obliged him at 2:00 a.m. that very next morning, so he set off for the schoolhouse.

Following his confession, Partridge lost his job as county engineer, although he protested that he had done nothing wrong as an engineer. After a thirty-day stay in a state mental hospital to assess his mental state (he was pronounced sane), he was convicted and sentenced to one to ten years for burning a school building and one to twenty-five years for burglary—the breaking and entering—sentences to run concurrently.

Since the school building had suffered about $4,100 worth of damages but was repairable, it was still where all black students in the first through sixth grades, by Hillsboro law, had to attend school. The building was still cold and drafty in the winter, run-down in general, and stocked with hand-me-down, outdated textbooks. And black children still had to walk to the Lincoln School from wherever they lived, even if one of the two white grammar schools—Webster and Washington—was much closer.

Partridge's sacrifice was not in vain, however. Black parents had been troubled by the educational inequalities for some time, and between the epic *Brown v. Board of Education* ruling and Partridge's bold move, they were finally galvanized to action. They petitioned the board of education for the right to attend the better schools but were told that the schools in question were too crowded. They needed to wait until the planned new set of grammar schools was built in 1956 or 1957.

A few black students showed up at the "white" schools anyway, and for a few days that seemed to be working until a sudden "school zoning"—Hillsboro's first, which involved some very creative mapping—placed 90 percent of all black students in town back at good old Lincoln and not a single white child there.

Although it was later proved that crowding was not really an issue, since the school district had in fact lost as many students that year as it would gain from allowing the blacks in, cynics noted that if twenty or thirty new white students suddenly materialized seeking admittance to these schools, room would have been found for them.

At this point the National Association for the Advancement of Colored People (NAACP), which had been watching a number of cities in Ohio for a strong opportunity to challenge the widespread segregation in the North as well as the South, lent its firepower to the integration effort.

Let us consider for a minute Hillsboro itself—the setting of what was to become the first lawsuit over segregation in the North after *Brown v. Board of Education.* The county seat of hilly Highland County in the southwestern part of the state, it was a prosperous rural town of a little more than five thousand people. Hillsboro was the place where farmers went to sell their produce and buy what they needed—all the roads in the area led into it like spokes to the hub of a wheel.

The town had a good selection of stores and a respectable number of small to medium-size manufacturing plants, including a bell foundry that made bells of all sizes used all over the country and the world. Its black population, as in many of the state's rural areas at the time, was low, less than 3 percent, so it was not the place one would most expect a racial issue. But as in many other places across the country, this black population was made to feel "its place," which was not one of equal footing. And now that was about to move from a subtle issue to a very public one.

In September 1954 five black mothers sued the Hillsboro school board and school superintendent Paul Upp for their alleged policy of segregation, seeking an injunction against the board's insistence that their children withdraw from the white schools of Washington and Webster and go back to the Lincoln school. The complicated legal battle that followed took two years to reach a resolution.

During that time, the quiet streets of Hillsboro saw a quiet revolution. Just about every school day, black parents led their children to the white schools and sent them in, only to have them sent right back out, refused admittance. Parents and children, some carrying signs that said things like OUR CHILDREN PLAY TOGETHER—WHY CAN'T THEY LEARN TOGETHER? would then head back home. At home, with the help of Quakers from nearby towns, the parents homeschooled their children.

Although there were occasional name-callings and racial slurs from onlookers, a few eggs tossed at cars, and at least one cross burned on a black family's lawn one night—called the act of "pranksters" by the local newspaper—there was no serious violence.

Meanwhile, on the legal front, the Cincinnati judge assigned to the case, John H. Druffel, did his best to avoid making a ruling, citing the fact that the Supreme Court had not yet indicated just how integration should be carried out. When the NAACP tried to force him to move forward via appeals, he encouraged them to take the case all the way to the Supreme Court. The Court declined the case, saying nothing had changed since *Brown v. Board,* forcing the case back into the arms of the court of appeals, which finally ordered "immediate integration."

The school board back in Hillsboro then did some stalling of their own, including waiting until they had the official order to integrate in their hands and insisting that all the former Lincoln School students be tested with materials not yet in hand. By the time this all came to pass, the 1955 school year had ended.

But by the beginning of classes in 1956, Hillsboro's grammar schools were totally integrated. As one white person who was in grammar school then remembers it, "The door opened one day, a janitor shoved in some desks, and we had black schoolmates."

Philip Partridge's night mission eventually achieved a great deal. Not only did it precipitate integration in the town he lived in, but it also prodded towns across the state, and in fact the country, to take steps toward ending segregation. They did not wish to be pilloried in the press along with Hillsboro.

Partridge didn't have to serve all those years in prison, by the way. He was such a model prisoner that he was paroled after nine months and was given a pardon by the governor years later when he asked for one. He did leave Hillsboro sometime after the incident, since finding work became difficult and his son took some flak from classmates over it all.

Interviewed when living again in Hillsboro in his nineties, Partridge said, "Setting fire to the school, it had to be done. I have no regrets, ever."

In 2004 a historical marker was erected at the site of the old Lincoln School, and in 2003 Philip Partridge's family received a plaque from the National Underground Railroad Freedom Center, citing him as "an example of a modern-day freedom conductor—a great example of courage in pursuit of justice and equality."

RENDEZVOUS AT THE ZOO

1957

It was a crisp April night at the Columbus Zoo—quiet, as most such places are after all the visitors and their little ones have gone home. A twenty-five-year-old part-time keeper, studying to be a veterinarian in his other life, crept up to a very special set of cages in the Johnson Aquarium, the ones with ¾-inch steel bars that housed one of the zoos' star attractions—male and female lowland gorillas captured in the wild by a Columbus adventurer and purchased by the zoo at great expense. He, like everyone else on the zoo staff, was well aware that the zoo's superintendent, Earle Davis, had given strict orders that these two be kept carefully apart. They were far too valuable to risk the aggression they'd shown toward each other the few times a tête-à-tête had been attempted.

Gorillas, the largest living primates, were certainly intimidating. The males, like the one pacing behind the bars here, could weigh up to 450 pounds; had an eight-foot arm span, huge canines, and tremendously powerful jaws; and looked in general like an unbelievably muscular man leaning forward on his knuckles. And thanks to *King*

Kong, and scores of poorly informed movies and novels before that, gorillas had a reputation for fierceness and viciousness that they truly did not deserve.

Keeper Warren Thomas was curious—or maybe he felt a little sorry for these prisoners in solitary confinement. In his evening rounds of feeding and cleaning around the massive creatures, he'd noticed some interactions between them that, despite the barriers keeping them apart, looked suspiciously like flirtation to him. So he took a chance—a *big* chance. When no one else was paying attention, he let the big male, Baron Macombo, and the smaller female, Millie Christina, spend some time together. At least once, that time was all night.

Warren didn't tell anyone about these secret rendezvous, although as the months passed and the playful little rituals seemed to have ceased, he wondered if the female could possibly be pregnant. With a portly gorilla, it's a little hard to tell. He was torn between 'fessing up and waiting to see if the zoo received a huge surprise some months from now. If the gorillas actually did produce a baby, it would be nothing less than worldwide news. By the early twentieth century, the zoos of the world finally had some gorillas that survived capture in the forests of Africa and subsequent captivity, and they of course wanted to breed them. But no zoo, no matter how large or knowledgeable, had any idea of how to accomplish this. Up to this point, no zoo had ever had a gorilla become pregnant.

So when Warren finally walked into Mr. Davis's office to confess his little crime, Davis was too thrilled to reprimand him. After a while, when nothing happened to negate the possibility, the news was cautiously let out that the Columbus Zoo might be expecting a baby gorilla early in the new year. Zoos across the nation and around the world were interested but skeptical. The Columbus Zoo was only a small zoo and not even the top zoo in Ohio—how could they possibly have achieved such a breakthrough?

As fall became winter, the gorilla watch was on in earnest. Would Millie put Columbus on the atlas of zoodom? No one in the world even knew how long a gorilla's gestation period was.

On the morning of December 22, eight and one-half months after she conceived, that question was answered. As Warren was feeding the gorillas that morning, he noticed that Millie was off her feed and acting strangely. When his eyes fell to the floor he saw a tiny gorilla there—still encased in its amniotic sac. He feared a stillbirth at first, until he saw the baby twitch. Since Millie seemed to be ignoring her baby, Warren snatched it up and ran for the kitchen of the gorilla house.

After he removed the sac, he cut and clamped the umbilical cord, massaged the newborn gorilla all over, and gave it mouth-to-mouth resuscitation. After a few minutes, its feeble attempts to breathe became sturdy and regular. Soon, like so many other young rescues of the animal world, it was sitting in a nest of rags within a cardboard box, sipping formula right next to a heater.

Like most human newborns, the miniscule gorilla, a female, was no beauty at first. Weighing less than four pounds at birth and only fifteen inches long, she was wrinkled and skinny. But soon she was a charming and venturesome little imp, and Columbus—and the country—went wild. Zoo visitation broke all attendance records. The mayor handed out cigars, and the city council (despite the grumbles of one councilman, who wondered "what these animals do when they are born in jungles") voted to provide the $11,000 Davis requested as emergency funds for a gorilla nursery. The gorilla had two full-time nursemaids—and soon more toys than the average day care center.

Telegrams, calls, and letters poured in to the zoo, and the tiny animal was on the front page of newspapers everywhere. The *New York Times* provided daily bulletins on her progress, and *Time* and *Life* magazines and TV programs like *I've Got a Secret* put her face into every living room. Zoos elsewhere wanted to rent her for $1,000 a day

(Davis refused), and scientists and behaviorists clamored to study her. For special occasions, the tot (which the zoo directors would like to forget) was dressed in frilly outfits, complete with bonnets.

Before long, the baby had a name as well. The zoo ran a contest, offering a $50 prize for the best name. Movie star Clark Gable, a native of Cadiz, about one hundred miles from Columbus, was so thrilled that his home state had pulled off such a coup that he added a $100 savings bond to the pot. The name Colo was finally chosen, a combination of Columbus and Ohio.

Colo, now at age fifty-four the oldest gorilla in captivity, still resides at the Columbus Zoo. She and her many progeny, and the many other gorilla-breeding firsts they achieved in later years, have done more than make Columbus a worldwide leader and expert in gorilla propagation. Colo and her offspring have helped improve the lot of zoo animals everywhere in general.

When renowned gorilla researcher Dian Fossey visited Colo and her mate, Bongo, at the zoo in 1983, she helped the zookeepers realize that gorillas and other captive animals needed more than secure cages, plenty of food, and occasional sex to have tolerable lives. One year after Dian's visit, gone were the ten- by fifteen-foot concrete-and-steel enclosures. The Columbus Zoo unveiled its new "gorilla villa"—a huge, multistory, open-air enclosure with plenty of things to climb and explore and play with, plus areas where the gorillas could escape from constant scrutiny. This was not quite the one to sixteen square miles of their range in the wild, but it was surely a step in the right direction.

As Louis DiSabato, the zoo's curator of mammals in 1956 put it, "Columbus is where it all started for gorillas. No matter what happens now or in the future, the zoo will always be remembered for Colo's birth." Go pay Colo and her handsome family a visit—the gorillas in Columbus are now into their fourth generation. You'll love the aquarium exhibits at the Columbus Zoo too.

"NOT A PARTICULARLY BAD FIRE!"

1969

Flames rose high, licking at the train trestle and the backs of the taverns that had been cantilevered over the river. The fire was a swathe only two hundred feet wide, but it ran for more than ten miles. The conflagration was fed by fuel oil, vegetable oil, gasoline, brush, and debris. Spectators lined the banks. The river itself was useless in fighting this fire—it was the river itself that was burning.

The Cuyahoga River fire of 1969 really didn't surprise Clevelanders. Nightclubs along the banks had patios that hung out over the river; somebody could have dropped a cigarette. Then there was the train trestle; a passing freight could have sent sparks into the river. One of the seagoing ships that plied the Great Lakes might even have sparked the fire as it passed through.

The fire chief pointed out that this "wasn't a particularly bad fire"; it wasn't even the worst fire on the Cuyahoga. In 1952 a similar fire caused $1.5 million dollars worth of damage. This one wouldn't be much more than $50,000. The difference was that all the previous fires had been local affairs. In 1969 the television and news media made a big deal out of this one.

The August 1, 1969, issue of *Time* magazine reported that the Cuyahoga River through Cleveland was "Some River! Chocolate brown, oily, bubbling with subsurface gases, it oozes rather than flows." That is how the world saw the eighty-five-mile-long Cuyahoga River as it meandered southward from Burton, Ohio, until it reached the Cuyahoga Falls, where it made a U-turn abruptly north before dumping into Lake Erie. To the rest of the world, the Cuyahoga became famous as "the river that caught on fire."

Cuyahoga is an Iroquois word meaning "crooked river." That aptly describes the way the Cuyahoga wanders through northeastern Ohio. For ten thousand years it drained the glacial flatlands from Akron to the Great Lakes. It became a landmark in 1795 as a demarcation for the Treaty of Green Ville that ended the Indian Wars in Ohio. For a brief time, it was effectively the western boundary of the United States.

Cleveland was founded in 1796 and served as a base for Commodore Oliver Hazard Perry during his epic battle with the British for control of the Great Lakes during the War of 1812. Then the Cuyahoga was a safe and heavily traveled waterway, carrying Native Americans and trade goods and providing drinking water for the numerous inhabitants along its banks. The Industrial Revolution changed all that.

Industrial plants arose on the shores of the Cuyahoga. Huge merchant vessels that plied the Great Lakes with their cargoes of oil, asphalt, salt, and iron ore made Cleveland a port of call. The mouth of the Cuyahoga River was cut four thousand feet east of its original course to allow for more and larger ships to traverse that part of the lake. They regularly dumped their ballast in the river. Steel mills rose on its banks, using the river's waters to cool their industrial plants and then dumping the oily waste back into the river.

The U.S. Army Corps of Engineers widened, drained, and straightened the channel, slowing the flow from the watershed. When the Ohio and Erie Canal opened, connecting the Ohio River and Lake Erie, the waters of the Cuyahoga were diverted to feed the canal system, further slowing the flow of this naturally lazy river. A scum of oil, municipal waste, twigs and branches, and old tires now floated down the river. Cleveland natives joked that if you fell into the Cuyahoga, you wouldn't drown—but you would immediately begin to decay!

Cleveland was all about industry. There were no regulations on how the waters of Lake Erie and the Cuyahoga were used. They seemed an inexhaustible resource. As far back as 1868, industrial effluent fed surface fires on the Cuyahoga. Fires erupted in 1883, 1887, 1912, 1922, 1936, 1941, 1948, and 1952. (There is a dispute as to whether the Cuyahoga has been on fire eight or thirteen times.) The river fire in 1969—one hundred years after the first—is the one that sparked the nation into action.

The Federal Water Pollution Control Administration rated the Cuyahoga as a "fire hazard," but it wasn't the only river in the country in trouble from pollution. Forty-three watersheds around the Great Lakes had been ranked as unsafe. Hundreds of streams across America had become unsafe due to industrial waste, and safe drinking water was not to be had in many riverfront communities. The public outcry caused by media attention was beginning to get the attention of politicians in Washington.

By 1969 the Cuyahoga was a "dead river." A Kent State University study showed water temperatures on average ten to fifteen degrees higher than normal around areas where wastewater was being dumped into the river. From Akron to Cleveland, the river had no living creatures—no fish, no plankton, not even water bugs! Wildlife migrated away from the river rather than drink its poison. The Kent State study said that the water was clear only to an inch at its headwater and then ranged from "gray-brown to rusty-brown" throughout its length.

Across the nation, newly formed environmental groups, scientists, and city fathers of towns along other polluted rivers raised a hue and cry to clean up and begin to protect our precious water sources. Then, on June 22, 1969, the Great Cuyahoga River Fire spurred the government into action.

Rachel Carson's book *Silent Spring* had caused important people to realize the need for federal government intervention to stop pollution. A series of other environmental disasters had occurred around the nation during the 1960s. The extent of the degradation of the environment was such that some local governments could not possibly rectify the damage on their own. In 1970 the Nixon administration, no tree-huggers, appointed William D. Ruckelshaus to establish the Environmental Protection Agency (EPA) with the stated mission, "to protect human health and the environment." The federal government appropriated billions of dollars to begin to clean up the rivers, the air, and the land that had been poisoned by industrial development.

Ohio soon followed with its own Ohio Environmental Protection Agency (OEPA). The state established the thirty-two-thousand-acre scenic Cuyahoga Valley Recreation Area (now Cuyahoga Valley National Park) and established rules for cleaning up the watershed and to penalize those who continued to abuse the environment.

Today there are fish again in the Cuyahoga River—and you can even eat them.

Looking back and considering the results, maybe the Cuyahoga River fire of 1969 "wasn't a particularly bad fire" after all.

THE KENT STATE CATASTROPHE

1970

Where a moment ago there had been the sound of jostling masses of protestors jeering at soldiers, there was now silence. It was a cold, shocked silence, the silence that the sight of the impossible brings. Indeed, something that ought to have been impossible happened on May 4, 1970. This was not Stalin's Russia, where people who dissented were lined up and shot. Yet there on the ground lay the dead bodies of four students, and after that stunned silence, the pained cries of others, wounded, filled the university green. This was not the work of some invading army, come to conquer. No, the shooters were National Guardsmen, and in thirteen fatal seconds they had gunned down four American university students and wounded at least nine others on the campus of Kent State University in idyllic Kent, Ohio. It was the beginning of the nationwide Student Strikes of 1970.

Kent State Normal School was founded in 1910 by Ohio Governor James M. Cox as one of two teacher training schools. The first 144 students graduated in 1914. By 1935 KSNS had grown to encompass several disciplines besides teaching. Governor Martin Davey, a longtime supporter of Kent State, signed a bill creating Kent State University. The student body increased manyfold when thousands of veterans returned to college from World War II, taking advantage of the new GI Bill.

Kent State was always a progressive school. As early as 1947 it offered the first tenured faculty position in the state to a young African-American professor, Dr. Oscar Ritchie. The beautifully manicured campus was a quiet, peaceful, pastoral setting. Things were about to change.

In 1969 Richard M. Nixon ran for president of the United States, promising to end the Vietnam War. So it came as a shock to students across America when, on April 30, 1970, after only four months in office, he announced that the United States was invading Cambodia. Protests erupted around the nation on the following day.

KSU students, like many others across the country, were opposed to the war. Ohio had a long tradition of antiwar churches and peaceful protests dating back to the Civil War. This invasion was seen as a betrayal of the trust many had placed in Nixon's promises, and KSU students gathered to discuss what actions could be taken to show their displeasure.

On May 1, the World Historians Opposed to Racism and Exploitation (WHORE) called for a rally on the campus commons to sign a petition opposing the war. The commons was a large grassy area in the middle of the campus that had traditionally been a place for students, faculty, and townsfolk to rally and voice dissent. A copy of the U.S. Constitution was set ablaze. Students burned their draft cards and called for the removal of the Reserve Officers' Training Corps (ROTC) from campus. Antiwar and anti-Nixon speeches went on for hours. Another rally was scheduled for the following Monday, May 4.

That night, students congregated around the bars on North Water Street in Kent, denouncing the war and demanding a pull-out from Cambodia. As a police cruiser made another pass observing the crowds, a bottle was launched at the police car, injuring two officers. Mayor Leroy Satrom ordered the bars closed, which only dumped more people into the streets. A brief scuffle broke out, windows were shattered, and a bonfire was built in the middle of North Water Street. The windows of the ROTC building on campus were broken out.

Because of the chaos, looting, and property damage, the mayor announced a state of emergency and asked Governor James A. Rhodes to send in the National Guard. The National Guard used tear gas to break up the gatherings. The FBI had warned city officials that violent, radical revolutionaries were descending on the town. Fifteen people, some of them students, were arrested and charged with disorderly conduct. The mayor declared a curfew from 8:00 p.m. to 6:00 a.m.

On the morning of May 2, the only Guardsman on campus was Lieutenant Barnette, who had been sent by Rhodes to assess the situation. By midday the ROTC building was on fire. Rhodes had campaigned on a platform of law and order and was no stranger to conflict. He authorized the Guard to take control of the campus and restore order. On May 3 he flew to Kent State Airport, where he berated the protesters as "un-American" and threatened to lock down the campus. He swore to use every force of law to restore order.

Nearly one thousand Guardsmen took control of the city, banning all demonstrations and rallies. The Kent State campus was placed under an even earlier curfew. Mayor Satrom and the president of the university would not meet with the students to address their demands. The students demanded the removal of the ROTC from campus and the right to vote.

The presence of the National Guard on campus heightened the tensions. That Sunday evening, protestors again engaged the police and Guardsmen with rocks and bottles. The authorities responded with tear gas and arrests.

Student leaders appealed to their fellow students to tone down their protests, and many returned to their dorms. The Guard took up positions in a few of the unused buildings. When the emergency measures invoked under the Riot Act became known, such as the suspension of civil rights and the right to assemble, angry students became violent. They tossed rocks and bottles at the Guardsmen and police. Again, tear gas and clubs were used to break up the crowds. Fifty-one students were detained for breaking the curfew.

On May 4 students held more rallies in direct contravention of police orders. Approximately three thousand people gathered on the commons; perhaps five hundred or so engaged in active protests. Across from the commons, one hundred armed Guardsmen surrounded the burned-out ROTC building. The National Guard tried to move the gatherings off the commons and Blanket Hill, another prominent gathering place on campus. Tear gas was launched at the students, who picked up the canisters and threw them back at the Guardsmen.

With bayonets at the ready, the Guardsmen advanced against the students. The students retreated up Blanket Hill, where they reorganized and pushed back. The National Guard was trapped between the students and the fenced-in football field. Students threw stones at the Guardsmen. A few Guardsmen made it to the top of Blanket Hill and turned toward the students. Shots rang out.

In thirteen seconds the Guardsmen fired between sixty-one and sixty-seven shots. Four students lay dead on the ground: protestors and antiwar activists Jeffery Glenn Miller, Allison Krause, and William Schroeder and Sandra Scheuer, a nonparticipant in the protests, who was shot while walking to class. Nine others were wounded.

The National Guard claimed they were under attack and under fire. FBI investigations later showed that at the time of the shooting, the student closest to the Guard was more than sixty feet away. Those killed were more that 270 feet away—two were more than 390 feet away. There was no evidence that students had been armed. Several civil and federal trials brought Guardsmen before the courts; all were acquitted of all charges.

The Kent State catastrophe was the beginning of a long, hot summer. Police clashed with students at twenty-six colleges. The National Guard was attacked on twenty-one campuses in sixteen states, and thirty ROTC buildings were burnt or bombed. Protests broke out in Washington, D.C., San Francisco, and New York. A cry rose up: "They can't kill us all."

President Nixon and authorities around the country felt that the nation was on the verge of a revolution. The president withdrew to Camp David with the 82nd Airborne for his own protection. Governor Rhodes closed Ohio's college campuses but permitted students to continue to attend classes at the residence of their professors so that they could finish the school year. Summer semesters were canceled.

Rhodes was ineligible to run for reelection but came back four years later to run for a third, then fourth term. When President Nixon signed the extension of the 1964 Civil Rights Act on June 22, 1970, he called for a constitutional amendment lowering the voting age. Ohio ratified the Twenty-sixth Amendment on June 30, 1971. The Constitution now gave eighteen-year-old citizens the right to vote in federal elections. On June 25, 1973, the Ohio Legislature lowered the voting age in local and state elections.

The following year, Kent State University founded a Center for Peaceful Change as a living memorial to those who died on that fateful day in May 1970. The university also offers a degree program for Conflict Studies and Conflict Resolution.

TO THE CELLAR!
(IF YOU HAVE ONE)

1974

In the Midwest the storms of spring and early summer are not just welcome rain, rumbling thunder, and an occasional bolt of lightning. In the back of your mind is always the unsettling thought of possible tornados—those fierce, frighteningly big funnels of wildly spinning air that appear suddenly and can leave havoc in their wake.

Ohio experiences an average of thirteen tornados a year, and though most of these do little harm, almost every Ohioan has heard those terrifying words "Head for the cellar" at least a couple of times in his or her life—and then done just that, perhaps snatching up a few cherished possessions and the family pets on the way.

In spring of 1974, however, meteorological forces were conspiring to multiply this dread scenario into an incredible, unprecedented extravaganza of weather woes—something scientists have come to call a "super outbreak." On April 3 a storm system developed that in just eighteen hours spawned 148 tornadoes across thirteen states, killing 315 people, injuring more than six thousand,

and causing $3.5 billion in property damage. How could such a thing have happened?

In short, a mass of cold, dry air moved toward the Midwest from the West, where it met moist, warm air coming up from the Gulf of Mexico. After a first series of thunderstorms, skies cleared long enough to heat the warm air even more, and the blanket of heavier cool air above it kept that air from rising. Soon that deadly set of forces, one type of air moving clockwise and the other moving counterclockwise, was set in motion—the phenomenon that gives rise to tornadoes. This particular storm system created not just scores and scores of lesser tornadoes but also an amazing total of twenty-four category F4s and six F5s. (Under the rating system scientists use to measure tornadoes, F5 is the worst possible.)

Of those F5s, with their potential for winds of more than three hundred miles an hour, the first and most formidable of all was the one that hit the quiet, unassuming little city of Xenia, Ohio. Xenia is located in southwestern Ohio, twenty miles east of Dayton, in the middle of a triangle formed by Interstates 70, 71, and 75.

The county seat of Greene County, Xenia was founded in 1803—the year Ohio was admitted to the Union—and its twenty-seven thousand inhabitants lived the life of the small-town Midwest, the life immortalized in the novels of Helen Hooven Santmyer (who was in fact a resident of Xenia) and Sinclair Lewis and the paintings of Norman Rockwell.

Their city was not spectacular or beautiful, but it had a few handsome buildings, its own proud history (including a name chosen at an early town meeting that means "hospitality" in Greek), and all the friendliness and optimism of the Midwest. A number of its residents were enthusiastic participants in the Underground Railroad before the Civil War, and by 1960 three rail lines of the literal kind—freight trains—served the city.

Xenia did not, however, have a tornado siren warning system, and the closest local weather stations—as was often the case in those days for reasons of cost—had no radar. So although the usual "severe thunderstorm alert" and "tornado watch" warnings had been issued periodically that afternoon by the national weather services, it was not until insidious signs appeared on the radar screens at Greater Cincinnati Airport in Covington, Kentucky, and the weather department of Dayton's TV channel WHIO that a direct warning was transmitted by teletype to Xenia's single radio station, WGIC. Soon the disc jockey was warning citizens to head for the cellar or lie down in the middle of an interior room and cover themselves with something sturdy.

Within minutes the tornado was at the door. It touched down at 4:40 p.m. nine miles southwest of the city and ripped its way northeast, plowing through several housing developments and the entire downtown. Seeming at times to break into more than one funnel, the tornado traveled a total of thirty-two miles until it wound down in nearby Clark County. By that time, 32 people were dead, 1,150 injured, and more than 40 percent of all the buildings in Xenia—both homes and commercial buildings—heavily damaged or destroyed.

Thousands of people were left homeless. The devastation in some areas was so great it was likened to the results of the saturation bombing of World War II. Hardest hit were the housing subdivisions of Arrowhead and Windsor Park, where many of the homes had no basements. But even basements were no guarantee against a storm of this force, which could blow the roofs and walls from even the sturdiest of frame buildings.

Among the casualties of the storm were nine of Xenia's churches and seven of its schools. Fortunately the storm hit after schools had been let out for the day, or the more than eight thousand students of the town might have been buried under rubble. The Kroehler manufacturing plant was destroyed, as were many other businesses and irreplaceable old residences. Seven cars were lifted from a moving freight train and sprinkled across downtown Xenia, and a tractor-trailer was blown across a street to the roof of the bowling alley on the other side.

After the tornado passed, rain started to fall on a world of roofless buildings, fallen trees, broken gas lines, scattered debris, crushed cars, and people wandering about in shock looking for help or lost loved ones. Children screamed and cried, and lost dogs scattered.

Help, however, was on the way. It streamed in from Wright-Patterson Air Force Base, only eleven miles away; the Air National Guard of Springfield, Ohio, hundreds strong; police from departments as far away as Troy and Wilmington; and the Red Cross, which was on scene within an hour. Doctors and nurses, many of them volunteers, rushed in from nearby city hospitals, and local contractors lent heavy equipment and manpower. Soon the area was a mass of ambulances, police cars, fire trucks, utility and tree service vehicles, dump trucks, bulldozers, and cranes; the flashers from all these vehicles lit the skies.

Soon also present were representatives of federal agencies such as the Department of Housing and Urban Development (HUD) and the Federal Disaster Assistance Administration and private organizations such as the Xenia Inter-Faith Council. Mennonites, many of them carpenters, arrived from all around Ohio to aid the cause. The U.S. Army Corps of Engineers removed unsafe buildings and eight hundred thousand cubic yards of debris. Last but by no means least, the insurance adjusters arrived with their straight faces and big checkbooks.

Politicians, including Ohio Governor John J. Gilligan, two U.S. senators from Ohio, and President Nixon, came also, from the very first night on, to comfort the citizens and promise the fastest and most complete aid the law would allow. Nixon (not yet fully to terms with Watergate) declared that this was the worst damage he had ever seen.

Less-welcome visitors included an endless stream of gawkers from nearby cities, who added to the at-times formidable road congestion in the area, and white middle-class looters in spiffy pickups looking for copper pipes and lumber and whatever else they could scrounge.

From the moment the roar of the tornado died away, the residents of Xenia had by and large shown an admirable spirit of helping themselves and moving forward—and so they did. An impressive plan for curing all the former ills of the city was proposed for the rebuilding, but it gave way in the end, as such things often do, to the forces of inertia and expediency. But Xenia was soon rebuilt—in time to be visited again, in 1989 and 2000, by more tornadoes. The 2000 tornado was an F4 that killed one person and injured a thousand. There had been earlier tornadoes, too, such as the one in 1933 that killed two and injured twenty-five.

Although the chances of a particular place being hit by a tornado are supposed to be one in 250, the Shawnee Indians, who called the land Xenia is built on "the place of the devil winds," may have had the right idea.

THE CHAMPIONS COME HOME

1976

It is hard to do justice to the thunderous joy in Cincinnati's historic Fountain Square on Friday, October 22, 1976. The red-uniformed Brookville Central High School Marching Band was pounding out "We are the Champions." Dozens of vendors were hawking the famous Cincinnati Skyline Chili Dogs. The streets of the city were strewn with tickertape, office-stationery confetti, and strips of toilet paper.

The paper had been falling from windows of the tallest buildings in town since the announcement that the Reds were coming down the street. Bob Braun, the TV celebrity from five-hundred-thousand-watt Clear Channel Station WLW, was squalling into a microphone that sent his words reverberating off the high walls of the central city canyons. As best he could, with his voice growing hoarse and fading, Braun shouted, "Cincinnati, here is your World Champion Big Red Machine."

The crowd of more than thirty thousand people bellowed their excitement as with one voice. Pete Rose had to step to the microphone, saying "Take it easy. We love you too! You're what makes this the baseball capital of the world." As Baseball Commissioner Bowie Kuhn came forward to hand the World Series Championship trophy to Sparky Anderson for the second time in two years, Sparky said, "Thanks again, Commish." The fans went wild.

This celebration was nothing short of pandemonium, but it was controlled chaos. Unlike in other cities, where celebrations like this often result in looting and property damage, these huge crowds were exuberant but friendly and orderly. Pete Rose was right. Cincinnati had the greatest fans in the world, and the Big Red Machine was the best baseball team to ever play the game.

The 1976 World Series was one of the most exciting in baseball history. The defending World Champion Cincinnati Reds were playing the winningest team in baseball, the New York Yankees. The National League Reds had defeated the Boston Red Sox to win the series in 1975. Now they were facing the legendary Yankees. The Yanks had won the World Series more than any other team in history.

The Reds' pitching lineup was second to none. The youngsters, Don Gullett and Pedro Borbón, backed up a veteran staff that included Gary Nolan and Jim Merritt. This was the first time the designated hitter was used in a National League ballpark. The pitchers would not bat, but that didn't matter. Manager Sparky Anderson's starting lineup included young men who had already become All-Stars. Johnny Bench, Pete Rose, Tony Perez, Lee May, Ken Griffey Sr., Joe Morgan, César Geronimo, and Bobby Tolan—most of them headed to the National Baseball Hall of Fame—gave the Reds power and depth.

The Yanks were no slouches either. Lou Piniella was hitting at a .394 rate and had an on-base average exceeding 71 percent.

Thurman Munson, Graig Nettles, Mickey Rivers, and Sandy Alomar had All-Star credentials.

No National League team had been World Champions two years in a row since 1922, so the sportswriters could be forgiven for discounting the Reds' chances.

The Reds had won the National League pennant by sweeping the Philadelphia Phillies in three games. Then they nailed down the World Series championship in a four-game sweep of the Yankees, only the second time ever that the Yanks had been swept. Shock-waves rolled through baseball. This was the first time in the history of the sport that a team had swept every postseason game. It was the BIG RED MACHINE.

The Cincinnati Reds were used to creating firsts in baseball. They became the first professional baseball team in the country when Harry Wright, a local jeweler, created the Red Stockings in 1869. In 1870 they won eighty-one straight games—a feat never again dupli-cated. At one point the Reds were barred from baseball because they sold beer at their stadium and wouldn't quit playing Sunday games.

They won the first "world series" in 1882. The Black Sox scandal of 1919 saw the Reds win the World Series, while the Chicago White Sox ended up having eight men barred from baseball forever for gam-bling on the game. (Gambling would soil baseball's reputation again in August of 1989, when the Commissioner of Baseball would bar the legendary Pete Rose from the Hall of Fame, and from baseball forever, for gambling on baseball games.)

The Reds were the first team to build their own stadium, Red-lands Field (later renamed Crosley Field) in 1912. In 1934 they were the first team to go to an away game by airplane. One year later, the first night game in the history of baseball was played under the lights at Crosley Field. Powel Crosley Jr. owned the local radio station,

WLW, and was the first to broadcast a live baseball game. In 1937 Johnny Vander Meer threw the first consecutive no-hitters in baseball. In 1944 the Reds hired pitcher Joe Nuxhall—at fifteen years of age, the youngest player ever in professional baseball. And in 1957 the Reds put its eight starters on the All-Star team, a feat still unmatched.

When Harry Wright formed his team in 1869, the game was pretty rowdy. There were no formal rules. Harry began to set clear standards: how many innings made a game, what constituted a home run, how many bases were really needed. Wright combined elements of cricket, rounders, and stickball to create a spectator sport—a sport that fans would pay to watch. He produced excitement in all the towns with "Double A" (Amateur Athletics) industrial teams. Paying customers brought out the entrepreneur in sportsmen. Boston hired away the Reds' best players and formed the Boston Red Sox. But Wright's Red Stockings came back to win 130 games in a row in the next two seasons.

As the league matured, baseball became America's game. During the "red" scares of the 1950s, when U.S. Senator Joe McCarthy was hunting Communists, the Reds prudently called themselves the Cincinnati Redlegs and replaced the "Reds" logo with a stylized "C" for Cincinnati. They didn't call themselves the Reds again until 1961.

Bob Howsam was general manager during the 1960s and deserved the credit for building a "farm system" that produced the Reds' best players. Howsam insisted on discipline—every Reds player was expected to be a role model parents could point to for their kids. Hair was kept short, beards shaved, no mustaches. The discipline paid off. By 1970 the team was poised to begin a dynasty.

Howsam hired George "Sparky" Anderson from San Diego where he had been a coach for only a year. Anderson's career had been undistinguished, but what Howsam saw was that Sparky could inspire players. Howsam wanted a manager to fire up the players and gave him the power to build a championship team. On June 30, 1970, the Reds moved to spacious new Riverfront Stadium, a fifty-two-thousand-seat palace of baseball on the banks of the Ohio River. The Reds won seventy of their first hundred games. Although 1971 was a disaster, Sparky made some key trades to beef up the team. In 1972 they won the National League West during the first-ever strike-shortened season, only to lose the World Series to the Oakland A's on a home run by Ohio native Gene Tenace.

The Reds took their third National League West crown of the young decade in 1973, only to lose the National League pennant to the New York Mets. In 1974 they finished behind the Los Angeles Dodgers. That year was notable for the heroics of the Atlanta Braves' Hank Aaron, who came into the Cincinnati series one homer shy of Babe Ruth's record. The Braves benched him, hoping to get the record in their own ballpark. When the commissioner ordered Atlanta to let him play, Aaron hit a booming long ball that just missed going over the wall. Two nights later in Atlanta, he popped number 714 out of the park.

The 1975 season was the stuff of legend. The Big Red Machine hit the field with Rose, Geronimo, Bench, Griffey, George Foster, Morgan, and Concepcion. The bullpen held six of the best pitchers in baseball, led onto the field by the young Don Gullett. The Reds won the National League West and then clubbed the Pittsburgh Pirates in three straight for the pennant. The next victim was the American League's Red Sox.

The Red Sox had to face both the Reds and the "curse of the Bambino," for having traded Babe Ruth to the Yankees. After seven hotly contested games, they fell to the Big Red Machine.

The Big Red Machine doubled up in 1976 to become the first National League team in forty-three years to win back-to-back World Series, beating the Yankees in a sweep. The Reds lineup batted over

.350 for the season, with Johnny Bench batting .533 with three homers and six RBIs during the series. They outscored the Yankees 22–8.

The 1975–76 Cincinnati Reds are often called the "best team ever to play baseball." They are the yardstick against which other great teams have been measured. After the 1976 season, Anderson and Howsam began to dismantle the Machine. The Reds owners fired Sparky Anderson, and Pete Rose moved on to Philly. Greats like Bench, Morgan, and Concepcion retired. Even as the Cincinnati Reds struggle to regain their prominence, Ohio baseball fans can never forget the powerhouse that was the Big Red Machine.

BICENTENNIAL BARNSTORM

1997

It was the fall of 1997, and Ohio's two-hundred-year anniversary—2003—was coming up fast. Bicentennial Committee member Nichola Moretti had a problem—a great idea and no clear way to implement it.

Nichola wanted to make everyone in the state aware of this big landmark moment and had finally hit on a way to do it: Turn one of the big staples of the Ohio landscape—the old wooden barns—into dramatic billboards. But traveling barn painters were a rare if not extinct species. The last Mail Pouch barn painter, Harley Warrick, had retired after painting his 20,000th barn in the famous black-and-yellow inducement to "Chew Mail Pouch Tobacco—treat yourself to the best."

Nichola was about ready to abandon her brainstorm when she happened upon a small-town newspaper whose front page proudly displayed a huge, neat, and colorful execution of the Ohio State University logo . . . on the front of a Belmont County barn.

Before he quite knew what happened, the artist of this opus—Scott Hagen—was sitting through some spirited meetings and heading for Columbus to sign a contract to paint one barn in every one of Ohio's eighty-eight counties.

Scott—a quiet, modest, competent, and polite young man of twenty-two—was as perfect an example of young Midwest manhood as Ohio's founding fathers could have conjured up. And believe it or not, he lived in town called Barnesville. After a little convincing by the Bicentennial Committee, he was more than willing to take on what many would have considered a daunting task. In fact he was looking forward to it—it was the sort of thing he'd been hoping to do all his life as an aspiring young artist.

He already had many of the skills called for in this odd undertaking—such as the ability to sketch even huge designs accurately freehand—but he was also lucky enough to live only twenty miles away from that cum laude Mail Pouch painter. From the elderly Harley, Scott learned such things as how to rig the sort of scaffolding that would be needed and how to adapt the scale of the logo to the size of a barn.

Then Scott hit the road on a five-year journey that would take him and his truck more than sixty-five thousand miles before he was through, use 645 gallons of paint, and wear out one hundred paintbrushes. (Only Sherwin-Williams paint—a product of Ohio—was used of course.)

First the barns were chosen, not by Scott but by the Bicentennial Committee, with the help of many not necessarily always impartial members of the public and barn enthusiasts. The barns selected for this august purpose had to be wooden, historic if possible, in decent condition, in an attractive setting, and above all, highly visible. The bigger a road they were on, the better. Ads in farm magazines solicited nominees, and barn-spotting and evaluating became a compulsive pastime for just about every member of the Bicentennial Committee.

Once the barns were picked, the owners, and often a swarm of volunteers from the nearby community as well, wore themselves out cleaning and repairing as needed in preparation for this great honor. Many of the barns were more than one hundred years old, and many had been built with great trees from the property they stood on. All once had been important parts of making a living in the new land called Ohio—and some still were. When the final cut was made, there were fifty-three white barns, twenty-nine red, five brown, and one yellow. Why the yellow one? The owner insisted: "My barn is yellow and it's going to stay yellow! My wife likes yellow, and it matches the house."

Although the designs Scott painted were much the same, with some interesting little variations here and there to suit the style of a particular barn or add a small custom touch for the owners, the barn-painting circuit did not lack for drama.

Just as he finished up barn #6 in Ottawa County in 1998, a tornado swept away the barn (along with a few of the neighbors' barns and even Scott's ladder). When Scott reached the halfway point, barn #44 in Union County, Governor Robert Taft joined him to lend a hand with the painting. And as he was painting the Clermont County barn in 2001, the terrifying news of 9/11 came through the radio headphones he often wore while painting.

As time passed, whenever Scott appeared in a county to start sketching that huge twenty- by twenty-foot bicentennial logo on a barn, he had more and more company. Interest in the project intensified over the years, and carloads, vanloads, even campers full of people would appear to watch his brushstrokes, perfectly happy to spend a day taking pictures and watching paint dry. Picnics and barbecues were held to celebrate the finishing of a barn, often complete with bands, speeches and fireworks.

It became a game, if not an obsession, to see how many of the completed barns you could visit. Motorcyclists, antique car clubs, school groups, Boy and Girl Scouts, and plain old tourists toured the hills, valleys, and plains of the state with their county barn score-cards. Bicentennial barn T-shirts, scrapbooks, posters, calendars, and miniatures proliferated. And upon the completion of the final barn in 2002, #88 in Sandusky County—a handsome Victorian structure and the only Bicentennial Barn to have the logo on its roof—there was a big bash worthy of the occasion, which not just the public but every Bicentennial Barn owner attended.

The Bicentennial Barn project didn't just add something interesting to the landscape. It also stirred state pride, kindled interest in history, and lent great impetus to the drive to preserve Ohio's wooden barns—a humble but irreplaceable part of the state's architectural heritage. The barns also gave everyone something charming and upbeat to focus on, in the all-too-often grim twenty-first century.

The owners of the Bicentennial Barns, some of whom had to be talked into participating in the project in the first place, are about as proud and determined a group of people as you could find—proud that their barns were chosen to signpost two centuries of statehood, and determined to keep them that way as long as possible. They have plans to keep the logos bright and attractive. They've planted flowerbeds beside their barns, lit them at night, and decorated them for Christmas and other holidays.

Bicentennial Barns are still the centerpiece for community gatherings of all kinds, including dances, picnics, hayrides, and pumpkin carvings. The owners of Butler County's Bicentennial Barn, whose place was swept by fire, lost their home, outbuildings, and just about all their possessions. But they were not devastated—their Bicentennial Barn had escaped the inferno.

With any luck these barns will be around for many more years to show future generations the result of sturdy barn raising and dedicated preservation efforts.

FOUND! THE BIGGEST BUCKEYE

2004

On May 21, 2004, a release from the Ohio Department of Natural Resources (ODNR) trumpeted the news: The biggest buckeye tree in the country was again firmly planted in the state where it obviously belonged—Ohio. As the triumphant ODNR chief of forestry put it, "We knew we had a big buckeye tree out there; it was just a matter of finding it. We are proud to have the national champion Ohio buckeye back in our state."

For the thirty years previous to this, Ohio had suffered the ignominy of seeing the largest specimen of their very own state tree located in Kentucky. Then an alert intern for the Ohio Division of Forestry spotted this monster—seventy-seven feet high, with a trunk "waistline" of 140 inches—near the village of Greenwich in Huron County, and the title was back where Ohioans knew it belonged.

It was not surprising that the biggest buckeye was in a front yard rather than the forest primeval, because National Champion Big Trees are usually found in places like yards, parks, and cemeteries, where they can grow in solo magnificence and spread their limbs in a way that would never happen amidst the close-hemmed competition of a full-scale forest.

Far more unusual, actually, is the fact that Ohioans in general would answer to the nickname of a rather obscure, usually middle-size understory tree—*aesculus glabra,* a relative of the horse chest-nut—that most of the bipedal "Buckeyes" today would not recognize if they stumbled upon it. How did this ever come about?

There is more than one account of the very first association of "buckeye" with "Ohioan." One is that when Captain Daniel of the Ohio Company first reached Point Harmar in the Ohio wilderness in April 1799, he cut the first tree felled by a settler west of the Ohio River—it was a buckeye.

A perhaps more plausible story, since settlers in the area probably cut trees earlier than 1799, ties the nickname to Ohio's first perma-nent white settlement of Marietta.

In September 1788 Indians of the Ohio Country were visiting the freshly minted town for treaty making. A grand parade of all the officials of the settlement was marching to the Campus Martius to open the first court. Col. Ebenezer Sproat, the newly appointed high sheriff, was one of those marchers, and his over six-foot-tall, hand-some, highly decorated figure—complete with vigorously brandished sword—so impressed the Indians that they exclaimed, "Heap big Hetuck!" Hetuck was their word for the fruit of the buckeye, a glossy brown nut with a large tan spot on it that is supposed to resemble a buck's eye. It is hard to get close enough to a live adult male whitetail to confirm this.

Fifty years later the buckeye bandwagon really got rolling. Wil-liam Henry Harrison, the hero of Tippecanoe, was running for president. Though born in Virginia, he had lived in and served the state of Ohio for most of his adult life and was living on a farm not far from Cincinnati at the time of the campaign of 1840.

Harrison's opponents claimed he was better suited to sitting in his log cabin drinking hard cider than steering the ship of state. When Harrison's party, the Whigs, called their national convention in Columbus, his supporters decided to turn this around to their advantage.

A little cabin of buckeye logs—there were plenty of buckeye trees on Harrison's farm—was built atop a wagon and decorated with buckeye nuts and coonskins. All the way to the convention, Otway Curry of Union County sat on the roof singing a song he'd composed, which called Ohio "the bonnie buckeye state." Harrison's supporters at the convention carried buckeye canes complete with dangling strings of buckeyes.

Soon rolling buckeye cabins and their attendant soundtrack had spread across the country. Though Harrison was hardly a humble frontiersman, all this log cabin and buckeye imagery captured the public imagination and helped propel him into the White House. He died there of pneumonia after a mere thirty-one and a half days in office, but the buckeye connection lived on.

Ohio State University in Columbus, whose more than fifty thousand students occupy the largest single campus in the United States, adopted the name Buckeyes for its sports teams, most notably its football team, which conjured up a giant animated buckeye called Brutus for its mascot. Brutus is a little dorky looking, but then, being a walking, talking tree nut isn't easy. The graduates of this sprawling intellectual city also proudly call themselves Buckeyes.

The Dawes Arboretum in Newark, Ohio, has buckeye trees planted in the shape of the number 17, lest we forget that Ohio was the seventeenth state to enter the Union.

What does a buckeye tree look like, you may wonder? You have probably seen its larger cousin, the horse chestnut (a native of the

Balkans), in city and suburban plantings. Though the horse chestnut is a much larger and taller tree, both it and the Ohio buckeye have distinctive compound leaves composed of five narrow leaflets that reach out from a central point like the outstretched fingers of a hand. The flowers are upright, branched clusters—yellow or greenish-yellow in the case of the buckeye versus the white of the showy horse chestnut.

Early settlers used the soft, light, easily shaped wood of the buckeye for trays, bowls, wooden spoons, paddles, and whistles, among other things. The wood is used less today but is still employed for objects from artificial limbs to packing crates to piano keys. Buckeye nuts were carried by early Ohioans to ward off rheumatism, and even now carrying one is supposed to bring good luck. Though buckeye nuts are considered at least somewhat poisonous to both people and livestock, Native Americans did eat them, cooked and mashed into meal. Wildlife, including squirrels and badgers, feast on them with impunity.

Returning to the subject of champion trees, Ohio had eleven national champions in the 2004–05 register, including a Norway maple, a Chinquapin oak, and a cucumbertree magnolia. That sounds impressive, until you stack it up against Florida's 163 champions, California's 102, and Arizona's 84.

This less than impressive showing is not too surprising when you consider Ohio's historical relationship with trees. A newcomer to the state is struck by its open spaces and is then astounded to discover that when the first white settlers arrived, Ohio was 97 percent forested. In its giant forests of oak, beech, hickory, sycamore, elm, ash, and tulip tree, it has often been noted, a squirrel could travel from one end of the state to the other without ever touching the ground. But by 1940 the nonstop chopping, hacking, and burning done by the pioneers and their descendants feverishly clearing land for crops had resulted in a state that was only 10 percent treed.

The gradual abandonment of small farms due to the Great Depression and the takeover of agriculture by agribusiness was actually good news for trees. By the late 1990s the state was back up to 33 percent forested, and growing.

The subject of tree ascendance ends on a happy note for Ohio. The largest tree in the entire United States, and in fact the largest living thing in the world, is a sequoia in California's Sequoia National Park named for an unforgettable Ohioan—General Sherman.

TWO WORLDS COLLIDE

2008

It was barely daylight on September 18, 2008, a beautiful time of year in the country, especially Amish country. But sprawled in the grass near the intersection of two roads in Hartsgrove Township, Ashtabula County, were the sad remains of yet another clash between the charming, anachronistic ways of the Amish and the full-speed-ahead, thoroughly mechanized twentieth and twenty-first centuries—an upturned cart, wheels askew; scattered books and other belongings; a dead horse; three boys groaning and thrashing in pain; and one seven-year-old who would soon be in the plain pine box the Amish use to bury their dead.

The four boys had set off that morning for their nearby Indian Creek School—Myron Miller, age seven, and his three brothers, who were nine, eleven, and thirteen. The boys were traveling down Windsor-Mechanicsville Road in an open pony cart when a late-model black van ran a stop sign and broadsided them.

The cart was flipped and tossed 150 feet onto the side of the road. A woman in a nearby home heard the crash and called 911 and then located the mother of the boys and brought her to the crash scene. The Amish mother's three older sons were soon on their way to Cleveland hospitals via Life Flight helicopter, where they were determined to be in critical condition, the result of serious injuries from which they are still recovering. As the helpful bystander noted for the news cameras, "A lot of lives were changed here in a flash, including that of the young man who hit them. He too will never be the same," she said of the driver of the van, a twenty-three-year-old man who was sitting by the side of the road, nearly hysterical.

Such accidents in Ohio are not uncommon. Although somehow "Pennsylvania Dutch Country" is what people think of first when the subject of "Amish" comes up, in fact Ohio is home to the world's largest population of "the plain people." The Amish migrated to Ohio in the early 1800s, and there are more than fifty thousand Amish in the state today (some estimates are over one hundred thousand), and steadily increasing. The Amish are most heavily concentrated in Holmes, Coshocton, Wayne, Richland, Geauga, and Trumbull Counties, but many other rural areas of the state have also sprouted the black-and-yellow "horse and buggy" outline signs that signify an Amish population nearby. The clippity-clop of horse's hooves and the creak of harnesses are heard on many a back road as the Amish go about their business, usually within 15 miles of their homes (which is about as far as a horse can travel, forth and back, in a day).

The Amish are the state's biggest noncommercial attraction— everyone loves to visit Amish country. Somehow the Amish symbolize the simplicity many of us secretly yearn for in the midst of our overcrowded, overcomplicated, overcommitted, and overscheduled lives. But with all the delights of Amish country—buggies, beards, straw hats, suspenders, bonnets, quilts, cheese, trail bologna, pretzels, and cinnamon buns, etc.—comes the very realistic problem of how fast, heavy metal motor vehicles and slow, lightweight wooden buggies can safely coexist.

In recent years the number of buggy–motor vehicle accidents in Ohio reached 140 a year, and depressing headlines highlighting the problem multiplied: 6 IN AMISH FAMILY KILLED AS TRUCK SLAMS A BUGGY; DRUNK DRIVER HITS AMISH BUGGY, SENDING AN AMISH MAN AND HIS FOUR YOUNG CHILDREN ALL TO THE HOSPITAL; AMISH BUGGY REAR-ENDED BY PICKUP, KILLING THREE AMISH TEENS; 5-YEAR-OLD AMISH GIRL IN CRITICAL CONDITION AFTER THE BUGGY IN WHICH SHE WAS RIDING WAS HIT BY A TANKER TRUCK.

In the uneven contest between cars and horse carts, the Amish were usually the ones injured, and their injuries were rarely minor ones. Finally, in 1999 the Ohio Department of Transportation and the Ohio Highway Patrol launched a serious study of the situation.

The report they published in 2000 was illuminating, and for the most part it pointed the finger very clearly at the "English," as the Amish call the rest of the world. Most car-buggy crashes occur in broad daylight and not at intersections or in adverse weather. The majority are caused by the failure of car drivers to realize the implications of the "speed differential." In other words, when the driver of a car going fifty-five miles per hour sees a buggy (going five to eight miles an hour) five hundred feet ahead and does not slow down, the car will hit the buggy within six and one-half seconds.

Other big reasons for car-buggy collisions include impatience on the part of local—not gawking tourist—motorists, often leading to illegal and reckless passing, and (shades of that overcomplicated life) distraction of car drivers by cell phones, CD players, beverage tending, and so on. Sun glare is another common culprit, as is failure to realize that horses are living and often flighty creatures. Then there is that other very un-Amish behavior, driving under the influence of alcohol and other mind-altering drugs. The man in the accident described earlier, for example, was later determined to have been driving while impaired by marijuana.

The report *Amish Buggy Safety in Ohio,* and the $7 million Amish Buggy Safety Program that followed, also had some good ideas for buggy drivers in the blizzard of posters, brochures, information sheets, billboards, meetings, and other attention-getters that followed.

Although most buggies today carry the triangular "Slow Moving Vehicle" reflector (first developed by Ohio State University, by the way), some of the most conservative orders of Amish are reluctant to be associated with anything in the gaudy colors of yellow, red, and orange, since their religion enjoins them to avoid calling attention to themselves in any way. For such sects, more Amish-friendly reflectors of white and gray have been developed. Many buggies today also have turn signals and feature battery-powered front lights and flashing rear lights for night use.

The report suggests adding white strobe lights atop buggies and perhaps tall flags such as those used by bicyclists, maybe even reflective bracelets and neckbands on horses. Buggies-only lanes, buggy overpasses over high-speed roads, and wider shoulders (so buggies can pull over to let cars pass) have also been suggested and sometimes implemented. A solar-powered or other nonelectric link between buggies and horse-and-buggy road signs has even been suggested so that the buggy signs will flash when a buggy is in the area. Driver education for buggy drivers and buggy registration have been considered, as has an age regulation for buggy drivers, who are sometimes out on the road by the age of eight.

In the end, the problem will probably be best solved by the simple practices of thoughtfulness and consideration. The Amish have truly mastered the principle of forgiveness. The most notable recent example of this was the astoundingly forgiving response of the Amish community of Nickel Mines in Lancaster County, Pennsylvania, to the man who invaded an Amish schoolhouse and shot ten Amish schoolgirls in 2006.

The Amish enrich all our lives, and they exhibit this same forgiveness at the scene of even the most dreadful vehicle accidents—usually not caused by them. In turn, we can show them some patience and awareness.

OHIO FACTS AND TRIVIA

Ohio 101

- Ohio is 225 miles wide and 210 miles north to south, for a grand total of 41,000 square miles.

- It is second in the United States in number of cities with a population of more than 500,000.

- It has 88 counties and 44,000 miles of rivers and streams.

- The name *Ohio* comes from the Iroquois for "great river."

Red, red, red!

The Ohio legislature probably never thought of this when establishing the various state standard-bearers, but Ohio has ended up with a very bold and stimulating color profile. The state bird (cardinal) is red, as are the state flower (red carnation), the state insect (ladybug), and the state beverage (tomato juice). Red also figures prominently in the state flag—the only swallowtail banner among the state flags—and at least ten colleges and universities in Ohio count red as one of their school colors. The state's top floriculture crop is the red poinsettia. Add in the facts that the largest ketchup bottler in the world is the Heinz plant in Fremont, Ohio, and that Ohio is the country's biggest producer of frozen pizzas, and Ohioans probably don't need to wear red power ties.

Creative thinkers and tinkerers

For a smallish state, Ohio has a lot of creative thinkers. Montgomery County, the county Dayton is the capital of, holds more patents per capita than any county in the entire country.

Here are just a few of the many things invented by Ohioans:

- The airplane, the cash register, the gas mask, and the electrolytic process that made mining aluminum practical

- The incandescent light bulb (and the many other things invented by Ohio-born Thomas Edison), the fluorescent tube light, arc lights, and the first electric traffic light

- The vacuum cleaner (and the disposable vacuum bag), disposable diapers, Freon, and Teflon

- Concrete street paving, safety glass, the spark plug, the tubeless tire, and the automobile self-starter

- Book matches, the Richter scale, and removable honeycombs (which revolutionized the beekeeping industry)

- The hot dog—maybe not the combination of frank and bun but that name for it—chewing gum, and Life Savers

- Rippled potato chips, compressed fresh yeast, the square-bottomed paper grocery bag, and the ice-cream cone rolling machine

- The beer can and the pop-top can

- Floating soap, and Preparation H

- The manure spreader and the mechanical corn picker

- The Thompson submachine gun, the Gatling gun, the clay pigeon, and the first pressurized space suit

- Live-virus polio vaccine, the creation of Albert Sabin

- Roller bearings and automatic railroad brakes

- The assembly line—which many believe really originated in the slaughterhouses of Cincinnati

- Play-Doh

- And innumerable other Ohio inventions too specialized, technical, or long obsolete to be included in this brief list

A fine array of firsts

It may have been the seventeenth state admitted to the Union, but Ohio has perhaps more than its share of firsts. These include:

- First dental school in the world, Bainbridge, 1827

- First black and first woman admitted to college in the United States, Oberlin College, 1837

- First woman to receive a degree from a medical college (and first in her class!), Elizabeth Blackwell, 1849

- First children's home in the country, Marietta, 1850s

- First recorded baby show, Springfield, 1854

- First black to be elected to public office in the United States, John M. Langston, Lorain County, 1855

- First war nurse, Mother Bickerdyke of Knox County, who set out in the 1860s to improve the nursing and living conditions of the Union wounded in the Civil War

- First train robbery in the United States, Ohio and Mississippi Line, North Bend, 1865

- First woman to graduate from dental school, Lucy Hobbs, Ohio College of Dental Surgery, Cincinnati, 1866

- First publicly broadcast weather forecast, Cincinnati, 1869

- First professional baseball team, the Cincinnati Reds, 1869

- First woman to run for president, Victoria Clafin Woodhull, 1872 First mass-produced toy (clay marbles), Akron, 1884

- First rubber tire, Akron, 1894–95

- First commercial chicken hatchery, New Washington, 1897

- First VFW post, Columbus, 1899

- First 4-H Club in the United States, started by A. B. Graham of Clark County in 1902

- First junior high school, 1909, and first kindergarten in the United States, both in Columbus

- First group of Boy Scouts of America, started by Daniel Beard of Cincinnati, 1910

- First gasoline filling station, Columbus, 1912

- First shot fired by an American in World War I, by Cincinnatian Robert Braley, 1914

- First major watershed district in the United States, the Miami Conservancy, 1915

- First National League football team, the Canton Bulldogs, 1920

- First use of a plane to dust crops, 1920s

- First air-conditioned railroad cars, 1930

- First Miss America (Mary Catherine Campbell), 1922

- First billionaire (and some say the richest man in history), John D. Rockefeller, 1930s

- First air-conditioned department store, the Lazarus Company, Columbus, 1934

- First 500,000-watt radio station in the world, WLW of Cincinnati, 1934

- First Alcoholics Anonymous meeting, Akron, 1935

- First Jeeps produced, Toledo, early 1940s

- First shopping center in the United States, Columbus, 1949

- First rock music concert, the Moondog Coronation Ball, held at the Cleveland Arena, 1952

- First microwave oven, produced by the Tappan Company of Mansfield, 1955

- First gorilla born in captivity, Columbus Zoo, 1957

- First U.S. astronaut to orbit the earth, John Glenn, 1962

- First woman to fly solo around the world, Jerry Mock, 1964

- First black mayor of a major U.S. city, Carl Stokes of Cleveland, 1967

- First man to walk on the moon, Neil Armstrong, 1969

- First woman in the United States to obtain a General Motors dealership and the first woman to purchase a major-league sports team—the Cincinnati Reds, in 1981—Margaret Schott of Cincinnati

- First municipal university, University of Cincinnati, 1819

- First TV talk show, Phil Donahue, WLWD-TV, Dayton, 1967

- First American woman rabbi ordained, Cincinnati, 1972

- First pet airline, Cincinnati, 1976

- First person to walk around the world alone, Steve Newman of Bethel, 1983–87

Ohio has the largest . . .

- Museum of military aviation in the world, the National Museum of the United States Air Force, Dayton

- Livestock exhibition in the United States, Ohio State Fair

- Manufacturer of glass in the world, Toledo

- Manufacturer of bicycles in the world, the Huffy Corporation of Dayton

- Single university campus in the United States, Ohio State University, Columbus

- Sandstone quarries in the world, Amherst

- Mastodon fossil ever discovered in the world, Clark County

- Man-made cavern in the world, Cincinnati Museum of Natural History

- Shoelace manufacturer in the United States, Mitchellace, Portsmouth

- Manufacturer of toy balloons in the world, Ashland

- Selection of roller coasters in the country, Cedar Point amusement park, Sandusky

- Roller coaster (longest and fastest) in the world, the Beast, Kings Island, Mason

- Soap manufacturer in the world, Proctor & Gamble, Cincinnati

- Trilobite fossil in the world, found in Montgomery County, 1988

- Single-breed horse show, American Quarter Horse Congress, Columbus

- Lawn mower in the United States, the Big Green Machine of Monroe, which mows an acre a minute

- Amish population in the world

- Pumpkin grown anywhere in the world, 1,725 pounds, produced in Jackson Township

- Water-powered gristmill in the United States, Clifton Mill in Greene County

- Exotic animal gamete bank in the United States, the Center for Reproduction and Endangered Wildlife, Cincinnati

- Bowling tournament in the country, the Hoinke Classic, Cincinnati

- Cuckoo clock in the world, Grandma's Alpine Homestead restaurant, Wilmot

- Half-dome building in the Western Hemisphere, Cincinnati's Union Terminal, built in 1933

- Bell manufacturer in the United States, the Verdin Company of Cincinnati

The oldest . . .

- Watercraft found in North America, a more than 3,500-year-old dugout canoe found in Ashland County

- University west of the Appalachian Mountains, Ohio University, Athens, founded in 1803

- College newspaper in the United States, the *Miami Student,* established in 1826

- High school football rivalry in the United States, Canton McKinley vs. Massillon

- Choral music festival in the United States, the May Festival, Cincinnati, first presented in 1873

- Municipal market in the United States, Findlay Market in Cincinnati

- Christmas bird count, started in 1900 in Harrison County

- Culinary arts festival (longest running) in the nation, Taste of Cincinnati

- Lighthouse operating on the Great Lakes, Marblehead, since 1922

- Gorilla in captivity, Colo, at the Columbus Zoo

Worst . . .

- School fire in the United States, the fire at the Collinwood School in Collinwood, 1908, in which 174 died, mostly children

- Hospital fire in the United States, the Cleveland Clinic Fire, 1929, which killed 123

- Prison fire in the United States, the Ohio Penitentiary Fire, 1930, Columbus, in which 322 inmates perished

- Nursing home fires in the nation, in Fitchville and Marietta, 1963 and 1970, killing 63 and 32 persons, respectively

- Mining accident in Ohio, the Millfield Mine explosion, 1930, in which 82 coal miners died

- Rail accident in Ohio, the collapse of the Ashtabula railroad bridge, 1876, in which 92 plunged to their death

- Airship disaster, the crash of the Navy dirigible *Shenandoah* in Noble County, 1925, which killed 14 and helped hasten the end of the airship era

- Maritime disaster involving Ohioans, the explosion of the steamboat *Sultana* on the Ohio River in 1865. (Built in Cincinnati, the ship was taking 2,300 freed Union POWs home when the boiler blew up, killing 1,700, many of them Ohioans.)

- Floods in Ohio, the 1913 flood, which killed more than 467 people across the state, and the Ohio River flood of 1937, which killed more than 250 in the river valley

- Tornado in Ohio, the Lorain Tornado of 1924, which killed 85 people

- Snowstorm in Ohio, the blizzard of 1978, in which 51 Ohioans died

Boys in blue . . . and gray

Ohio had quite a presence in the War Between the States. For just a hint of why this was so:

- All the winningest Northern generals—Grant, Sherman, and Sheridan—were Ohio born and raised. George Armstrong Custer was also an Ohioan.

- Ohio was third in the number of soldiers it provided, but it actually contributed more for its size than any other state in the North. Three out of every five men between the ages of eighteen and forty-five went off to serve. Between combat and disease, almost 35,000 of these died. Ohio also had some of the youngest soldiers in the conflict, including Johnny Clem, the "drummer boy of Shiloh," and Gilbert Van Zandt.

- At least 19 Union generals, 53 brigadier generals, and 134 brevet generals were from Ohio. At least seven Confederate generals were from Ohio as well.

- John Brown, who did much to ignite the Civil War, was a native of Ohio.

- In 1863 Brig. Gen. John Hunt Morgan undertook the longest cavalry raid of the Civil War, intimidating twenty-two Ohio counties before his capture.

- When the Congressional Medal of Honor was instituted after the war, the first sixteen recipients were from Ohio.

Musical notes

- Cleveland and Cincinnati are among the mere seventeen cities in the United States to have full-time symphony orchestras.

- The term "rock and roll" was originated by Cleveland's WJW DJ Alan Freed.

- The Rock and Roll Hall of Fame in Cleveland has a jukebox with more than 25,000 tunes

- Ohio songwriter Daniel Emmett wrote not just the unforgettable tune "Dixie," but old-time favorites like "Turkey in the Straw," "Blue Tail Fly," and "Old Dan Tucker."

- Rev. Benjamin Hanby of Westerville composed "My Darling Nellie Gray," and "Up on the Housetop."

- Stephen Foster, a native of Pennsylvania, composed "Oh! Susanna" and "Old Folks at Home" during his years in Cincinnati.

- The Ohio state song is "Beautiful Ohio."

- The state rock song is "Hang on Sloopy," composed by Rick Derringer and first recorded by the McCoys of Dayton.

- Henry Mancini, the composer of "Moon River" and "Pink Panther Theme," among many others, was born in Ohio, as was bandleader Sammy Kaye.

- Some of the better known Ohio songbirds include Teresa Brewer, Rosemary Clooney, the Isley Brothers, Dean Martin, the McGuire Sisters, the Mills Brothers, Johnny Paycheck, and Lil' Bow Wow.

Buckeye broadcasting biggies

- The Voice of America, an important force for the free world, was broadcast from Butler County, Ohio, from 1944 to 1994. Thus Hitler was one county off when he referred to "those Cincinnati liars."

- Lowell Thomas, the famous news correspondent and adventurer, was from Woodington, Ohio.

- Ted Turner, founder of the Cable News Network (CNN), was born in Cincinnati.

Movie stars and other performers

Born and/or bred in the Buckeye State:

- Theda Bara

- Halle Berry

- William Boyd (Hopalong Cassidy)

- Joe E. Brown

- Drew Carey

- George Chakiris

- George Clooney

- Tim Conway

- Director Wes Craven

- Doris Day

- Phyllis Diller

- Marie Dressler

- Clark Gable

- Teri Garr

- Lillian and Dorothy Gish

- Joel Gray

- Margaret Hamilton

- Anne Heche

- Bob Hope (a Clevelander from the age of 4)

- Burgess Meredith

- Paul Newman

- Sarah Jessica Parker

- Jack Paar

- Tyrone Power

- Roy Rogers, "King of the Cowboys"

- Martin Sheen

- Producer/director Steven Spielberg

Writers

The long roll call of writers who were born in, lived in, and/or were inspired by Ohio includes:

- Sherwood Anderson

- Ambrose Bierce

- Earl Derr Biggers, creator of the Charlie Chan novels

- Steven Birmingham

- Erma Bombeck

- Louis Bromfield

- Bruce Catton

- Hart Crane

- Rita Dove

- Paul Dunbar

- Alan Eckert

- Harlan Ellison

- Nikki Giovanni

- Zane Gray

- Walter Havighurst

- Fannie Hurst

- Josephine Johnson

- William H. McGuffey, author of the seven "readers" that became the most commonly used school textbooks in the 1800s, selling a total of 120 million copies

- Toni Morrison

- O. Henry

- Norman Vincent Peale

- Joseph Ray, creator of the arithmetic "word problem"

- James Reston

- Helen Steiner Rice, the "poet laureate of greeting card verse"

- Conrad Richter

- Helen Hooven Santmyer

- Arthur Schlesinger Jr.

- Benjamin Spock

- Gloria Steinem

- Harriet Beecher Stowe

- James Thurber

Artcetera

- The best-known artists of Ohio include Thomas Cole, John Quincy Adams Ward, Frank Duveneck, Elizabeth Nourse, George Bellows, Henry F. Farney, Philip Hale, Archibald M. Willard, John Ruthven, James Werlane, and Maya Lin, designer of the Vietnam War Memorial.

- The popular cartoon strips *Terry and the Pirates* and *Steve Canyon* were the brainchildren of Milton Caniff of Highland County.

- Superman was created by Jerome Siegel of Cleveland.

- The popular penmanship system known as Spencerian script was created by Platt R. Spencer of Geneva in the nineteenth century.

- The Greater Cincinnati Airport (located in northern Kentucky!) and the Union Terminal in Cincinnati house an impressive array of Art Deco mosaics depicting Ohio scenes.

- In conjunction with Cincinnati's bicentennial, artist/architect/ designer Andrew Leicester created a massive sculpture of three smokestacks (symbolizing Cincinnati's industrial strength), each topped with an enormous winged pig. Cincinnatians embraced the image, holding a fund-raiser for the arts in 2000 called the "Big Pig Gig." Artists from all over the country created flying pig artworks that sold for a total of more than $800,000,which was used to support local art projects.

Political peculiarities

- Ohio has sent more men to the White House than any other state except Virginia: William Henry Harrison, Ulysses S. Grant, Rutherford B. Hayes, James A. Garfield, Benjamin Harrison, William McKinley, William Howard Taft, and Warren G. Harding.

- Benjamin Harrison is the only grandson of a former president to ever be elected president.

- Ohio has long been a bellwether state in politics—no Republican has ever been elected president without winning Ohio.

- Nancy P. Hollister was the first woman governor of the state—for all of eleven days—in 1999.

- The first radio broadcast by a president was by Warren G. Harding.

- The originators of the Easter egg roll on the White House lawn were Rutherford B. Hayes and his wife, Lucy.

- An Ohio governor, James A. Campbell, introduced the system of voting by secret ballot.

- Ohioans immortalized on U.S. currency: Ulysses S. Grant ($50 bill), William McKinley ($500 bill), and Salmon P. Chase ($10,000 bill; no longer issued).

- The Sherman Anti-Trust Act of 1890 was originated by General Sherman's brother, Senator John Sherman.

- Clarence Darrow, the champion of separation of church and state in the famous Scopes trial of Tennessee, was a native of Kinsman, Ohio.

- In 1836 a war between Michigan and Ohio over Ohio's northern border (and the port of Toledo) was narrowly averted by the intervention of President Andrew Jackson.

A few fun festivals

Ohio, like most other states, has a hefty list of fairs and festivals of every kind every year. To whet your appetite, here are just a few of the more unusual ones, some of them unique to the Buckeye State:

- Banana Split Festival, Wilmington: a '50s and '60s celebration featuring the drugstore where this delicacy is supposed to have been invented (although Latrobe, Pennsylvania, claims this same invention)

- Bucyrus Bratwurst Festival

- Circleville Pumpkin Show, Circleville: now one of the nation's largest festivals; pumpkin everything in all shapes and sizes, complete with pumpkin-shaped water tower

- Coshocton Hot Air Balloon Festival

- Dandelion May Fest & Great Dandelion Cook-off, Dover

- Moonshine Festival, New Straitsville

- Northeast Ohio Polka Fest, Geneva-on-the-Lake

- Octoberfest Zinzinnati: the second largest such event in the world after the original one in Munich, Germany

- Ohio Pawpaw Festival, Albany

- Polar Bear Plunge, Geneva

- Flake by the Lake (flint-knapping festival), Van Buren

- Feast of the Flowering Moon, Chillicothe

- Olde Canal Days Festival, Canal Fulton

- Port Clinton Walleye Festival

- Avon Heritage Duct Tape Festival

- Pork Rind Heritage Festival, Harrod

- Father of All Duck Races (rubber ducks, that is), Greenfield

- Pro Football Hall of Fame Festival, Canton

- Southern Ohio Storytelling Festival, Chillicothe

- Sunflower Festival, Evendale

- Sweet Corn Festival: at least five of them in Ohio; the best-known is in Fairborn

- Twins Days, Twinsburg

- Woolybear Festival, Vermilion

A tiny taste of the Ohio oddities worth seeing

The back roads as well as the cities of Ohio have plenty of one-of-a-kind sights and attractions. Here is a tiny sample of some of the more obscure.

- The seven-story Longaberger Basket headquarters building in Newark, built as a giant replica of one of their best-selling baskets

- The more than 130 covered bridges still in use in Ohio

- The 52 elaborate murals on the floodwalls of Portsmouth, illustrating the history of the county

- The collection of more than 70,000 buttons, all different, in Dover

- The collection of more than 100 swallowed objects in the Allen County Museum

- The giant rubber stamp sculpture by Claes Oldenburg and Coosje Van Bruggen, in Willard Park, Cleveland

- The stone castle in Loveland, built by hand with stone from the riverbed of the Little Miami by a "knights of old" enthusiast

Agricultural notes

- Three of Ohio's most notable agricultural inventions: the Rome Beauty apple, the Poland China hog, and tomatoes designed for ease of processing, known affectionately as Ohio 7814 and 7810

- The latter did a lot to make Ohio the second largest producer of processing tomatoes in the nation.

- Ohio is the top producer of Swiss cheese and Liederkranz cheese in the United States, and its top income crops in 2008 were corn, soybeans, milk, poultry and eggs, and hogs.

- In 1841 Cincinnati had 62 slaughterhouses and 48 pork-packing companies, in case you ever wondered why one of its early nicknames was "Porkopolis."

- In 1850 Ohio was the top agricultural state in the nation; today agriculture accounts for less than 10 percent of the gross state product.

Other products to be proud of

- Flint from Flint Ridge in Licking and Muskingum Counties was the first choice of area Native Americans for arrow- and spearheads.

- Ohio produces more Japanese auto parts and trucks than any other state.

- Ohio is the third largest producer of salt in the nation. There is enough still salted away in the ground of northern Ohio to supply the entire United States for more than 30,000 years.

- The high-quality sand of northern Ohio made Toledo one of the glass-producing giants of the world.

- Ohio clay has likewise given places like East Liverpool the title of "the pottery capital of the world."

- The Akron area has long been known as the "rubber capital of the world" for the many rubber products it has invented and produced.

- Ohio is also a heavy hitter in the manufacture of machine tools, iron, and steel.

- It is first in the nation in the production of that unassuming but important mineral, limestone.

Nature notes

- John Aston Warder founded the American Forestry Association while living near Cincinnati. The Forestry Congress in that city in 1882 began the tradition of Arbor Day.

- In 1914 Martha, the last known living American passenger pigeon, died in the Cincinnati Zoo. The passenger pigeons of the American Midwest were originally the most numerous bird species in the world.

- A pretty tame place now, Ohio once had timber wolves, elk, mountain lions, lynx, and bison along with its wild turkeys and white-tailed deer.

- Ohio has its very own weather forecasting groundhog, named Buckeye Chuck, who resides in Marion. His forecasts don't always agree with Punxsutawney Phil's in Pennsylvania.

- The Wisconsin Glacier, which once covered two-thirds of the state, was an estimated 8,000 feet deep at its thickest point, near Cleveland. The scrapes the glacier left on the limestone of Kelley's Island in Lake Erie are the most dramatic such geologic traces in the world.

Weather woes

- The coldest temperature so far recorded in Ohio was negative 39 degrees, at Milligan, in 1899.

- The highest recorded temperature is 113 degrees, at Thurman in 1897 and Gallipolis in 1934.

- On July 11, 1900, a hailstorm at Elyria produced hailstones more than three inches in diameter.

- Anna, Ohio, has experienced more than forty earthquakes since 1875, including one that was the worst ever in Ohio, measuring 5.5 on the Richter scale.

- The blizzard of 1978 stranded more than 5,500 people on Ohio's roadways, and resulted in more than 100 million dollars worth of damages, mostly killed livestock and milk that couldn't make it to market.

Bad apples in the Buckeye State

- Charles Manson was born in Cincinnati.

- Jeffrey Dahmer spent much of his childhood in Bath.

- Public Enemy #1, Pretty Boy Floyd, was killed near East Liverpool by federal agents in 1932.

- John Dillinger, another top bad guy, shot the sheriff of Lima in 1933.

- In 1938 Anna Marie Hahn was the first woman executed in Ohio's electric chair. She poisoned five elderly people to support her gambling habit.

- In 1975 James Ruppert of Hamilton committed America's largest family mass murder, eleven victims.

- In 1992 serial sniper Thomas Lee Dillon of Canton was sentenced to 165 years in prison.

A sampling of Ohio sports superstars

Baseball: Coaches Branch Rickey and Walter Alston; players Cy Young, Pete Rose, Miller Huggins, Roger Bresnahan, Ed Delehanty, Mike Schmidt, Steve Yeager, Buck Ewing, Jesse Haines, Elmer Flick, Rube Marquand, George Sisler, Leroy "Satchel" Paige, Ben Johnson, Frank Robinson, Phil and Joe Niekro, Ken Griffey Jr., and Roger Clemens; Kenesaw Mountain Landis, the first commissioner of baseball

Basketball: Coach Bobby Knight; players John Havelicek, Jerry Lucas, Bill Hosket, Nate Thurmond, Nate Archibald, and LeBron James

Football: Coaches Woody Hayes, Paul Brown, Ara Parseghian, and John Heisman; players Roger Staubach, Don Schula, Larry Cszonka, Paul Warfield, Lou Groza, Dante Lavelli, Cliff Battles, Marion Motley, Bill Willis, Clarke Hinkle, George McAfee, Joe Carr, Wilbur Henry, Len Dawson, Jack Lambert, Alan Page, and Mike Michalske

Track stars: Olympic Hall of Famer Jesse Owens, "the Buckeye Bullet," who single-handedly demolished the myth of Aryan superiority at the 1936 Olympics; Edwin Moses, Olympic gold medalist

Golf: Jack Nicklaus

Archery: Olympic gold medalist Darrell Pace

Figure skating: Olympic champion Scott Hamilton

Horse racing: Jockey Eddie Arcaro

Boxing: Ezzard Charles and James Jeffries, world heavyweight champions; Rat "Boom Boom" Mancini, world lightweight champion

Auto racing: Barney Oldfield

BIBLIOGRAPHY

The Mystery Beneath the Mystery

Adams County Visitors Guide, produced and edited by Tom Cross and the Adams County Travel & Visitor's Bureau. West Union, OH: *The People's Defender,* 2009.

Baskin, John, and Michael O'Bryant, eds. *The Ohio Almanac: An Encyclopedia of Indispensable Information About the Buckeye Universe,* 3rd ed. Wilmington, OH: Orange Frazer Press, 2004.

Crawford, Brad, and William Manning, photographer. *Ohio: An Insider's Guide.* New York: Compass American Guides, 2005.

Glotzhober, Robert C., and Bradley T. Lepper. *Serpent Mound: Ohio's Enigmatic Effigy Mound.* Columbus: Ohio Historical Society, 1994.

Goodman, Rebecca, and Barrett J. Brunsman. *This Day in Ohio History.* Cincinnati, OH: Emmis Books, 2005.

Hansen, Michael C. "The Serpent Mound Disturbance." *Timeline,* September/October 1998.

Heinrichs, Ann. *America the Beautiful: Ohio.* New York and Danbury, CT: Children's Press, 1999.

Lepper, Bradley T. "Great Serpent." *Timeline,* September/October 1998.

Parker, Geoffrey, Richard Sisson, and William Russell Coil. *Ohio the World 1753–2053: Essays Toward a New History of Ohio.* Columbus: Ohio State University Press, 2005.

Stille, Sam Harden. *Ohio Builds a Nation: A Memorial to the Pioneers and the Celebrated Sons of "the Buckeye State,"* 4th ed.

Lower Salem, OH, Chicago, and New York: The Arlendale Book House, 1953.

Willis, James A., Andrew Henderson, and Loren Coleman. *Weird Ohio: Your Travel Guide to Ohio's Local Legends and Best Kept Secrets.* New York: Sterling Publishing, 2005.

Woodward, Susan L., and Jerry N. McDonald. *Indian Mounds of the Middle Ohio Valley: A Guide to Mounds and Earthworks of the Adena, Hopewell, Cole, and Fort Ancient People.* Blacksburg, VA: The McDonald and Woodward Publishing Company, 2002.

http://en.wikipedia.org/wiki/Asteroid_belt

http://en.wikipedia.org/wiki/Meteorite

http://en.wikipedia.org/wiki/Serpent_Mound

A Trip to the Indian Arsenal

Converse, Robert N. *The Archaeology of Ohio.* Archaeological Society of Ohio, 2003.

"Flint Ridge Gives Up Secret of Ancient Tribe of Aborigines," *Newark Advocate,* August 25, 1919.

"Flint Ridge Tells Story of Earliest Ohio Inhabitants," *Newark Advocate,* May 13, 1927.

Hatcher, Harlan. *Buckeye Country: A Pageant of Ohio.* New York: H. C. Kinsey & Company, 1940.

Hurlburt Jr., Cornelius S. *Minerals and Man.* New York: Random House, 1970.

"Indian Princess Relates History of Flint Ridge," *Newark Advocate,* December 14, 1966.

Peacefull, Leonard, ed. *A Geography of Ohio.* Kent, OH: Kent State University Press, 1996.

"Primitive Man for Centuries Obtained His Weapons Here," *Newark Advocate*, June 20, 1933.

Romain, William F. *Mysteries of the Hopewell: Astronomers, Geometers, and Magicians of the Eastern Woodlands.* Akron, OH: The University of Akron Press, 2000.

White, Jon Manchip. *Everyday Life of the North American Indian.* New York: Indian Head Books, 1979

www.artcom.com/Museums/nv/af/43739-96.htm

http://en.wikipedia.org/wiki/History_of_Ohio

www.eskimo.com/~knapper/a_day_at_the_ridge.htm

http://findarticles.com/p/articles/mi_qa3904/is_200104/ai_n8941369/

www.ohiodnr.com/geo/flint/tabid/11702/Default.aspx

www.ohiohistorycentral.org/entry.php?rec=1283

www.ohiohistorycental.org/entry.php?rec=1361&nm=Flint

www.ohiohistorycentral.org/entry.php?rec=2217

http://ohsweb.ohiohistory.org/places/c01/index.shtml

www.nps.gov/history/mwac/hopewell/v1n1/eleven.htm

The Birth of Tecumseh

Bond, Beverley W., Jr. *The Foundations of Ohio.* Columbus: Ohio State Archeological and Historical Society, 1941.

Cayton, Andrew R. L. *Ohio: The History of a People.* Columbus: Ohio State University Press. 2003.

Edmunds, David R. *Tecumseh and the Quest for Indian Leadership.* Boston: Little, Brown and Company, 1984.

Hatcher, Harlan. *Buckeye Country: A Pageant of Ohio.* New York: H. C. Kinsey & Company, 1940.

Knepper, George W. *Ohio and Its People*. Kent, OH: Kent State University Press, 2003.

The Mighty Chieftains, by the editors of Time-Life Books. Alexandria, VA: Time-Life Books, 1993.

Waldman, Carl. *American Indian History to 1900,* rev. ed. New York: Checkmark Books, 2001.

Massacre at Gnadenhutten

Baker, Colleen. "Gnadenhutten." A paper presented October 1, 2003, at Wilmington College, Wilmington, OH.

Barr, Daniel P., ed. *The Boundaries Between Us: Natives and Newcomers Along the Frontiers of the Old Northwest Territory, 1750–1850*. Kent, OH: Kent State University Press, 2006.

Knepper, George W. *Ohio and Its People*. Kent, OH: Kent State University Press, 2003.

www.moravian.org/history

www.ohiohistorycentral.org

A Royal Christening

Campus Martius and Ohio River Museum; (740) 373-3750.

Hulbert, Archer Butler. *The Records of the Proceedings of the Ohio Company,* Vol. I. Marietta, OH: Marietta Historical Society, 1917.

Knepper, George W. *Ohio and Its People*. Kent, OH: Kent State University Press, 1989.

Washington County Historical Society; (740) 373-1788.

White, Larry Nash, and Emily Blankenship White. *Images of America: Marietta*. Charleston, SC: Arcadia Books, 2004.

Wolf, Glenn. Telephone interview, November 20, 2009. According to Glenn Wolf, a researcher at the Washington County Historical Society, the bell at Campus Martius was ordered by Mrs. Rufus Putnam, wife of one of the Ohio Company of Associates investors. He claims there is no evidence that Marie Antoinette had anything to do with the bell. Wolf says that he has seen documents that indicate that Col. John May of the Ohio Company contacted his father-in-law, Joseph May, on Mrs. Putnam's behalf and asked that the bell be cast. That, according to Wolf, is the bell at Campus Martius. As a side note, Joseph May was the grandfather of Louisa May Alcott.

http://en.wikipedia.org/wiki/American_pioneers_to_the_ Northwest_Territory

http://en.wikipedia.org/wiki/Marietta,_Ohio

www.ohiohistorycentral.org

St. Clair's Shame

Edmunds, R. David. *Tecumseh and the Quest for Indian Leadership*. Boston: Little, Brown and Company, 1984.

Knepper, George W. *Ohio and Its People*. Kent, OH: Kent State University Press, 2003.

Sugden, John. *Blue Jacket: Warrior of the Shawnees*. Lincoln: University of Nebraska Press, 2000.

Sugden, John. *Buckongahelas in American National Biography*. New York: Oxford University Press, 1999.

The Battle of Fallen Timbers

Barr, Daniel P. *The Boundaries Between Us: Natives and Newcomers along the Frontiers of the Old Northwest Territory, 1750–1850*. Kent, OH: Kent State University Press, 2006.

Boyer, Paul, et al. *The Enduring Vision,* 6th ed. Boston: Houghton Mifflin Company, 2008.

Eckert, Allen. *The Frontiersman.* New York: Bantam Books, 1967, 1981.

Kappler, Charles J. *Treaty with the Wyandot—1795.* Lincoln: University of Nebraska Press, 1903.

Knepper, George W. *Ohio and Its People.* Kent, OH: Kent State University Press. 2003.

Raccoons Build a Bookshelf

Baskin, John, and Michael O'Bryant, eds. *The Ohio Almanac: An Encyclopedia of Indispensable Information About the Buckeye Universe,* 3rd ed. Wilmington, OH: Orange Frazer Press, 2004.

"The Coonskin Library," *Athens Messenger,* December 21, 1875.

Cutler, Sarah J. "The Coonskin Library." *Ohio History,* Vol. 26, March 8, 2005.

Directory of Ohio Libraries. State Library of Ohio, 2008.

Havighurst, Walter. *Ohio: A History.* Urbana and Chicago: University of Illinois Press, 2001.

The Land We Call Ohio: 88 Counties, 88 Paintings, 88 Histories. Project coordination and editing by John W. Hoberg, profiles by Deborah Bradford Linnville, paintings by Richard M. Canfield. Columbus, OH: Paint Ohio, LLC, 2003.

www.americanprofile.com/heroes/article/4454.html

www.amesvilleohio.org

http://oak.cats.ohiou.edu/~deanr/coonskin.html

www.ohiohistorycentral.org/entry.php?rec=692

http://omp.ohiolink.edu/OMP/Subject?subject=literary

The Great Apple Planter Arrives in Ohio

Haley, W. D. *"Johnny Appleseed: A Pioneer Hero,"* as first published in *Harper's Monthly Magazine,* 1871. Sandwich, MA: Chapman Billies, Inc., 1994.

Hatcher, Harlan. *The Buckeye Country: A Pageant of Ohio.* New York: H. C. Kinsey & Company, 1940.

Hope, James, and Susan Failor. *Bountiful Ohio: Good Food and Stories from Where the Heartland Begins.* Bowling Green, OH: Gabriel's Horn Publishing, 1993.

Lawlor, Laurie. Wood engravings by Mary Thompson. *The Real Johnny Appleseed.* Morton Grove, IL: Albert Whitman & Company, 1995.

Moses, Will. *Johnny Appleseed: The Story of a Legend.* New York: Philomel Books, 2001.

Price, Robert. *Johnny Appleseed: Man & Myth.* Urbana, OH: Urbana University Press, 1954, 2001.

www.american folklore.net/folktales/oh.html

www.appleappetite.com/Johnny.htm

http://cleveland.about.com/od/peopleandpets/p/johnnyappleseed.htm

http://en.wikipedia.org/wiki/Johnny_Appleseed

www.nativetreesociety.org/historic/johnny_appleseed_tree.htm

www.ohiohistorycentral.org/entry.php?rec=94

www.straightdope.com/columns/read/2141/whats-the-story-with-johnny-appleseed

"We Have Met the Enemy, and They Are Ours"

Bird, Harrison. *War for the West, 1790–1813.* New York: Oxford University Press, 1973.

Cayton, Andrew R. L. *The Frontier Republic: Ideology and Politics in the Ohio Country, 1780–1825.* Kent, OH: Kent State University Press, 1986.

Dillon, Richard. *We Have Met the Enemy: Oliver Hazard Perry, Wilderness Commodore.* New York: McGraw-Hill, 1978.

Garrison, Webb. *A Treasury of Ohio Tales.* Nashville: Rutledge Hill Press, 1993.

Knepper, George W. *Ohio and Its People.* Kent, OH: Kent State University Press, 2003.

www.brigniagara.org/battle.htm

http://en.wikipedia.org/wiki/Battle_of_Lake_Erie

www.ohiohistorycentral.org

The Great Groundbreaking

Ostrander, Steven, text, and Ian Adams, photographer. *Ohio: A Bicentennial Portrait.* San Francisco: BrownTrout Publishers, 2002.

Cayton, Andrew R. L. *Ohio: The History of a People.* Columbus: Ohio State University Press, 2002.

Davis, William I. *A History of Newark, Ohio, 1800–1869.* Newark, OH: Newark Public Library, 2007.

Hagerty, J. E., C. P. McClelland, and C.C. Huntington. *History of the Ohio Canals: Their Construction, Cost, Use, and Partial Abandonment.* Columbus: Ohio State Archeological and Historical Society, 1905.

Havighurst, Walter. *Ohio: A History.* Urbana and Chicago: University of Illinois Press, 2001.

Hill, N. N. Jr. *History of Licking County.* Newark, OH: Graham & Co. Publishers, 1881.

Knepper, George W. *Ohio and Its People.* Kent, OH: Kent State University Press, 2003.

Montgomery, Janine, and Kathy Akers. *Let's Discover Ohio. Student's Edition.* Kettering, OH: Schuerholz Graphics, 1995.

Ohio Trivia, rev. ed. Compiled by Ernie and Jill Couch. Nashville, TN: Rutledge Hill Press, 1992.

Perry, Dick; photography by Bruce Goldflies. *Ohio: A Personal Portrait of the 17th State.* Garden City, NY: Doubleday & Company, 1969.

Scheiber, Harry N. *Ohio Canal Era: A Case Study of Government and the Economy.* Athens: The Ohio University Press, 1987.

Stille, Sam Harden. *Ohio Builds a Nation: A Memorial to the Pioneers and the Celebrated Sons of "the Buckeye State,"* 4th ed. Lower Salem, OH, Chicago, and New York: The Arlendale Book House, 1953.

The Land We Call Ohio: 88 Counties, 88 Paintings, 88 Histories. Project coordination and editing by John W. Hoberg, profiles by Deborah Bradford Linnville, paintings by Richard M. Canfield. Columbus, OH: Paint Ohio, LLC, 2003.

Wilcox, Frank. *The Ohio Canals.* Selected and edited by William A. McGill. Kent, OH: Kent State University Press, 1969.

http://americanhistory.suite101.com/article.cfm/the_decline_and_ rebirth_of_the_ohio_erie_canal

http://americanhistory.suite101.com/article.cfm/the_ohio_erie_ canal

http://en.wikipedia.org/wiki/Akron,_Ohio

http://en.wikipedia.org/wiki/De_Witt_Clinton

http://en.wikipedia.org/wiki/Miami_and_Erie_Canal

http://my.ohio.voyager.net/~lstevens/canal

www.ohiohistorycentral.org/entry.php?rec=753

www.ohiohistorycentral.org/entry.php?rec=2158&nm=Erie-Canal

www.ohiohistorycentral.org/entry.php?rec=2348

www.rootsweb.ancestry.com/~ohwarren/Bogan/bogan373.htm

www.touring-ohio.com/day-trips/ohio-erie-canal.html

Troubled Bridges Over the Waters

Georgano, G. N. *The Beaulieu Encyclopedia of Automobiles*.
London: Taylor & Francis Group, 2002.

Knepper, George W. *Ohio and Its People*. Kent, OH: Kent State
University Press, 2003.

www.ohiohistorycentral.org

www.ohionationalroad.or/s-bridge.htm

On Thin Ice

Blight, David W., ed. *Passages to Freedom: The Underground
Railroad in History and Memory*, Washington, D.C.:
Smithsonian Books, 2004.

Bordewich, Fergus M. *Bound for Canaan: The Underground
Railroad and the War for the Soul of America*. New York:
Amistad Books, 2005.

Coffin, Levi. *Reminiscences of Levi Coffin, the Reputed President of
the Underground Railroad*. Cincinnati: Western Tract Society,
1876.

Hagedorn, Ann. *Beyond the River: The Untold Story of the Heroes of
the Underground Railroad*. New York: Simon & Schuster, 2002.

Havighurst, Walter. *Ohio: A History*. Urbana and Chicago:
University of Illinois Press, 2001.

Stowe, Harriet Beecher. *Uncle Tom's Cabin*. Pleasantville, New York: Reader's Digest Association, 1991. Original edition 1852.

The Land We Call Ohio: 88 Counties, 88 Paintings, 88 Histories. Project coordination and editing by John W. Hoberg, profiles by Deborah Bradford Linnville, paintings by Richard M. Canfield. Columbus, OH: Paint Ohio, LLC, 2003.

Tobin, Jacqueline L. *From Midnight to Dawn: The Last Tracks of the Underground Railroad*. New York: Doubleday, 2007.

Young, Paul. *The Underground Railroad's Busiest Escape Route*. Hillsboro, OH: Paul Young, 2004.

http://en.wikipedia.org/wiki/John_Rankin_(abolitionist)

http://en.wikipedia.org/wiki/Margaret_Garner

http://en.wikipedia.org/wiki/Underground_Railroad

www.johnparkerhouse.org/?q=taxonomy/term/8

www.ohiohistorycentral.org/entry.php?rec=3098

http://ohsweb.ohiohistory.org/places/sw14/index.shtml

www.sojust.net/poems/watkins_eliza_harris.html

www.suite101.com/article.cfm/the_underground_railroad/107684/2

http://utc.iath.virginia.edu/interpret/exhibits/turner/turner.html

http://wishc.mnsi.net/heritageroom/elizaharris.htm

The Grim Fate of the *Griffith*

Great Lakes Shipwreck Disasters. Kenosha, WI: Southport Video. One-hour video.

Kohl, Cris. *100 Best Great Lakes Shipwrecks,* Vol. I. West Chicago, IL: Seawolf Communications, 1998.

Proceedings of a Meeting and Report of a Committee of the Citizens of Cleveland in Relation to Steamboat Disasters on the Western Lakes. Cleveland: Steam Press of Harris, Fairbanks, and Co., 1850.

Ratigan, William. *Great Lakes Shipwrecks and Survivals.* Grand Rapids, MI: Wm. B. Eerdmans Publishing Company, 1960.

Reynolds, Francis E. *Griffith: Smoke on the Waters.* Alpena, MI: Sarge Publications, 1997.

Ritchie, David. *Shipwrecks: An Encyclopedia of the World's Worst Disasters at Sea,* 2nd ed. New York: Facts on File, 1999.

Wachter, Georgann and Michael. *Erie Wrecks East: A Guide to Shipwrecks of Eastern Lake Erie,* 2nd ed. Avon Lake, OH: Corporate Impact, 2003.

www.alcheminc.com/asht.html

http://clevelandcivilwarroundtable.com/articles/biography/balthasarbest.htm

www.divethegreatlakes.com/search/wreckDive.php?id=1785

http://ech.cwru.edu/ech-cgi/article.pl?id=MD

http://files.usgwarchives.net/oh/newspapers/tidbits/tbs39.txt

http://halinet.on.ca/Greatlakes/Documents/HGL/default.asp?ID=s044

www.rootsweb.ancestry.com/~ohlcgs/willoughby/griffith.html

www.steamboats.org/desaster-htmls/9070.htm

www.wepl.lib.oh.us/OLD/Wick_History/Wick_History.htm

West Point or a Pony?

Clinton County Historical Society, Wilmington, OH.

Historical Marker Application. Ohio Historical Markers Program, Attachment 1. Columbus: Ohio Historical Society, 1998.

Keesee, Dennis M. *Too Young to Die: Boy Soldiers of the Union Army*. Huntington, WV: Blue Acorn Press, 2001.

Little Sure Shot Gets Started

Akers, Kathy, and Janine Montgomery. *Let's Discover Ohio*. Kettering, OH: Schuerholz Graphics, 1995.

Booth, Stephane Elise. *Buckeye Women: The History of Ohio's Daughters*. Athens: Ohio University Press, 2001.

Kasper, Shirl. *Annie Oakley*. Norman: University of Oklahoma Press, 1992.

Royster, Jacqueline Jones. *Profiles of Ohio Women 1803–2003*. Athens: Ohio University Press, 2003.

www.bookrags.com/eb/oakley-annie-eb/

http://en.wikipedia.org/wiki/Annie_Oakley

http://girlscantwhat.com/oakley-annie-sharpshooter/

www.trivia-library.com/b/biography-of-sharpshooter-annie-oakley

An Intemperate Temperance Woman

Cayton, Andrew R. L. *Ohio: The History of a People*. Columbus: The Ohio State University Press, 2002.

Compton's Interactive Encyclopedia. Elmhurst, IL: Encyclopedia Britannica, Inc., Online.

Dannenbaum, Jed. *Drink and Disorder: Temperance Reform in Cincinnati from Washingtonian Revival to the WCTU*. Urbana: University of Illinois Press, 1984.

Kerr, Austin K. *Organized for Prohibition: A New History of the Anti-Saloon League*. New Haven, CT: Yale University Press, 1985.

Knepper, George W. *Ohio and Its People*. Kent, OH: Kent State University Press, 2003.

www.biographybase.com

www.ohiohistorycentral.org

Ohio Gives Flight to the World

Cayton, Andrew. *Ohio: The History of a People*. Columbus: Ohio State University Press. 2002.

Howard, Fred. *Wilbur and Orville: A Biography of the Wright Brothers*. New York: Knopf, 1987.

Knepper, George W. *Ohio and Its People*. Kent, OH: Kent State University Press, 2003.

www.daytoninternationalairport.com/history

www.nasa.gov/centers/glenn/about/bios/ohio_astronauts.html

www.ohiohistorycentral.org/entry.php?rec=424

The Con Woman of Millionaires' Row

The Encyclopedia of Cleveland History. Bloomington: Indiana University Press, and Cleveland: Case Western University, electronic edition, July 23, 1997.

http://en.wikipedia.org/wiki/Cassie_Chadwick

http://freepages.genealogy.rootsweb.ancestry.com/

www.onlinebiographies.info

The Drowning of Dayton

Baskin, John, and Michael O'Bryant, eds. *The Ohio Almanac: An Encyclopedia of Indispensable Information about the Buckeye Universe*, 3rd ed. Wilmington, OH: Orange Frazer Press, 2004.

Goodman, Rebecca, and Barrett J. Brunsman. *This Day in Ohio History*. Cincinnati, OH: Emmis Books, 2005.

Hatcher, Harlan. *Buckeye Country: A Pageant of Ohio*. New York: H. C. Kinsey & Company, 1940.

Havighurst, Walter. *Ohio: A History*. Urbana and Chicago: University of Illinois Press, 2001.

Knepper, George W. *Ohio and Its People*. Kent, OH: Kent State University Press, 2003.

Schmidlin, Thomas W., and Jeanne Applehans Schmidlin. *Thunder in the Heartland: A Chronicle of Outstanding Weather Events in Ohio*. Kent, OH, and London: Kent State University Press, 1996.

Stille, Sam Harden. *Ohio Builds a Nation: A Memorial to the Pioneers and the Celebrated Sons of "the Buckeye State,"* 4th ed. Lower Salem, OH, Chicago, and New York: 1954.

The Writers Program. *The Ohio Guide*. State of Ohio. Part of the Federal Writers Project, 1940.

http://en.wikipedia.org/wiki/Great_Dayton_Flood

www.ohiohistorycentral.org/entry.php?rec=694

Ohio's Onion Field War

Knepper, George W. *Ohio and Its People*. Kent, OH: Kent State University Press, 2003.

Rumer, Tom. *Unearthing the Land: The Story of Ohio's Scioto Marsh*. Akron, OH: University of Akron Press, 1999.

Williams, Mardo. *My Accidental Career*. New York: Calliope Press, 2009.

http://en.wikipedia.org/Hardin_County_onion_pickers_strike

www.waymarking.com/waymarks/WM2H76_Village_of_
McGuffey_Great_1934_Onion_Strike_Marker_15_33

The Nadir of Elliott Ness

Badal, James Jessen. *In the Wake of the Butcher: Cleveland's Torso Murders*. Kent, OH: Kent State University Press, 2001.

http://en.wikipedia.org/wiki/Cleveland_Torso_Murderer

http://en.wikipedia.org/wiki/Eliot_Ness

http://en.wikipedia.org/wiki/Serial_killer

A Storybook Setting Comes to Life

Bacall, Lauren. *By Myself and Then Some*. New York: Harper Entertainment, 2005.

Bacall, Lauren. *Now*. New York: Alfred A. Knopf, 1994.

Bubbeo, Daniel. "Humphrey Bogart: To Have and Have Not": http://bogart-tribute.net/bio.shtml.

Carter, John T. *Louis Bromfield and the Malabar Farm Experience*. Mattituck, NY: Amereon House, 1995.

Cayton, Andrew R. L. *Ohio: The History of a People*. Columbus, OH: Ohio State University Press, 2002.

Goodman, Rebecca, and Barrett J. Brunsman. *This Day in Ohio History*. Cincinnati, OH: Emmis Books, 2005.

Hatcher, Harlan. *Buckeye Country: A Pageant of Ohio*. New York: H. C. Kinsey & Company, 1940.

Knepper, George W. *Ohio and Its People*. Kent, OH: Kent State University Press, 2003.

Sperber, A. M., and Eric Lax. *Bogart*. New York: William Morrow and Company, Inc., 1997.

The Land We Call Ohio: 88 Counties, 88 Paintings, 88 Histories. Project coordination and editing by John W. Hoberg, profiles by Deborah Bradford Linnville, paintings by Richard M. Canfield. Columbus, OH: Paint Ohio, LLC, 2003.

Wilkinson, Christina. *Bicentennial Barns of Ohio: A Tribute to the Barns and Their Owners.* Mentor, OH: Rosewood Press, 2003.

www.dnr.state.oh.us/tabid/762/Default.aspx

http://en.wikipedia.org/wiki/Humphrey_Bogart

http://en.wikipedia.org/wiki/Lauren_Bacall

Putting a Match to Prejudice

Cross, Kris. "Highland County Woman Recalls Growing up During the Height of Segregation," *The People's Defender*, West Union, OH, January 22, 2003.

"Did Brown Matter?" *The New Yorker*, May 3, 2004.

Hillsboro Press-Gazette. Coverage of all stages of this event and its aftermath, 1954–1956.

"Holdout in Ohio." *Time,* April 23, 1956.

Howard, Shelly. "Through Brown-Colored Glasses: Desegregation in Hillsboro, Ohio." Research paper. Bowling Green University.

Howard, Shelly. *Community Crusaders: Desegregation in Hillsboro.* Videotape. 2002.

Obituary of Philip Partridge. *Highland County Press,* May 25, 2003.

Pack, Charlotte. Series of articles on this subject written for the *Highland County Press* in 2003.

Summary of this subject written up by the African American Awareness Research Council, for the application for a historical marker at the site, May 16, 2003.

Williams, Steven. "The School Fight of 1954: Desegregation of the Hillsboro City Schools." Paper written for Ohio History 303, Wilmington College, 2004.

www.ohiohistorycentral.org/entry.php?rec=1585

www.ohiohistorycentral.org/entry.php?rec=1944

www.wilmington.edu/about/news/4496/5556/no

Rendezous at the Zoo

Fossey, Dian. *Gorillas in the Mist.* London: Hodder and Stoughton, 1983.

Goodman, Rebecca, and Barrett J. Brunsman. *This Day in Ohio History.* Cincinnati, OH: Emmis Books, 2005.

Lyttle, Jeff. *Gorillas in Our Midst.* Columbus: Ohio State University Press, 1997.

Nichols, Michael, photographs and essays. *The Great Apes: Between Two Worlds.* Contributions by Jane Goodall, George B. Schaller, and Mary G. Smith. Washington, D.C.: The National Geographic Society, 1993.

http://en.wikipedia.org/wiki/Colo_(gorilla)

http://en.wikipedia.org/wiki/Dian_Fossey

http://en.wikipedia.org/wiki/Gorilla

http://endangered-species.suite101.com/article.cfm/the_lowland_gorilla

www.dispatch.com/live/contentbe/dispatch/2006/11/12/20061

www.history.com/this-day-in-history.do?action+VideoArticle&…

www.ohiohistorycentral.org/entry.php?rec=2224

BIBLIOGRAPHY

"Not a Particularly Bad Fire!"

Knepper, George W. *Ohio and Its People.* Kent, OH: Kent State University Press, 2003.

"Some River." *Time*, August 1, 1969.

www.epa.gov/history/timeline/index.htm

www.ohiohistorycentral.org/entry.php?rec=1642

The Kent State Catastrophe

Hensley, Thomas. *The Kent State Incident: Impact of Judicial Process on Public Attitudes.* Westport, CT: Greenwood Press, 1981.

Lewis, Jerry M., and Thomas R. Hensley. "The May 4 Shootings at Kent State University: The Search for Historical Accuracy." *The Ohio Council for Social Studies Review,* 34, no. 1 (1998): 9–21.

Palmer, James. "Outline of the Events at Kent State University, May, 1970." Wilmington College, 2009.

Sorvig, Kim. *To Heal Kent State: A Memorial Meditation.* Philadelphia: Worldview Press, 1990.

Whitney, R. E. *The Kent State Massacre.* Charlotteville, NY: SamHar Press, 1975.

To the Cellar! (If You Have One)

Laffoon, Polk IV. *Tornado: The Killer Tornado That Blasted Xenia, Ohio, in April 1974.* New York: Harper & Row Publishers, 1975.

Schmidlin, Thomas W., and Jeanne Applehans Schmidlin. *Thunder in the Heartland: A Chronicle of Outstanding Weather Events in Ohio.* Kent, OH, and London: Kent State University Press, 1996.

www.3.gendisasters.com/ohio/7975/xenia-oh-terrible-tornado-
apr-1974

www.april31974.com/The_storm.html

http://en.wikipedia.org/wiki/Super_Outbreak

http://en.wikipedia.org/wiki/Xenia, Ohio

www.idreamof.com/disaster/1974_xenia.htm

www.ohiohistory.org/etcetera/exhibits/swio/pages/content/
1974_tornado.htm

www.ohiohistorycentral.org/entry.php?rec=1615

www.xeniatornado.com/

The Champions Come Home

Neft, David S., and Richard M. Coen. *The World Series,* 1rst ed.
New York: St. Martin, 1990.

http://en.wikipedia.org/wiki/The_Big_Red_Machine

http://en.wikipedia.org/wiki/Cincinnati_Reds

http://en.wikipedia.org/wiki/sam_wyche

http://en.wikipedia.org/w/index.php?title=1976_World_Series

www.naplesnews.com/newes/209/nov/05/mlb/johnny_bench

http://sportsillustrated.cnn.com/baseball/mlb/features/1997/
wsarchive/1975.html

Bicentennial Barnstorm

Gorczyca, Beth, photography by B. Miller. *Ohio's Bicentennial
Barns: A Collection of the Historic Barns Celebrating Ohio's
Bicentennial.* Wooster, OH: The Wooster Book Company,
2003.

Ohio Bicentennial 1903–2003: A Time to Celebrate. Video. Ohio
Bicentennial Commission, 2000. Produced by Jane Temple,

written by Michael Moore. A Production of EDR Media and Beechwood Studios.

The Land We Call Ohio: 88 Counties, 88 Paintings, 88 Histories. Project coordination and editing by John W. Hoberg, profiles by Deborah Bradford Linnville, paintings by Richard M. Canfield. Columbus, OH: Paint Ohio, LLC, 2003.

Wilkinson, Christina. *Bicentennial Barns of Ohio: A Tribute to the Barns and Their Owners.* Mentor, OH: Rosewood Press, 2003.

http://en.wikipedia.org/wiki/Mail_Pouch_Tobacco_Barn

www.ohiohistorycentral.org/entry.php?rec=1725

Found! The Biggest Buckeye

Ostrander, Steven, text, and Ian Adams, photographer. *Ohio: A Bicentennial Portrait.* San Francisco: BrownTrout Publishers, 2002.

Everett, Thomas H. *Living Trees of the World.* New York: Doubleday & Company, Inc.

Hatcher, Harlan. *Buckeye Country: A Pageant of Ohio.* New York: H. C. Kinsey & Company, 1940.

Hope, James, and Susan Failor. *Bountiful Ohio: Good Food and Stories from Where the Heartland Begins.* Bowling Green, OH: Gabriel's Horn Publishing, 1993.

Kingsbury, John M. *Poisonous Plants of the United States and Canada.* Englewood Cliffs, NJ: Prentice-Hall, Inc., 1964.

Knepper, George W. *Ohio and Its People.* Kent, OH: Kent State University Press, 2003.

Little, Elbert L., photographs by Sonja Bulaty, Angelo Lomeo, and others. *The Audubon Society Field Guide to North American Trees, Eastern Region.* New York: Alfred A. Knopf, 1980.

Peacefull, Leonard, ed. *A Geography of Ohio*. Kent, OH: Kent State University Press, 1996.

Schonberg, Marcia, illustrated by Bruce Langton. *B is for Buckeye: An Ohio Alphabet*. Chelsea, MI: Sleeping Bear Press, 2000.

The Land We Call Ohio: 88 Counties, 88 Paintings, 88 Histories. Project coordination and editing by John W. Hoberg, profiles by Deborah Bradford Linnville, paintings by Richard M. Canfield. Columbus, OH: Paint Ohio, LLC, 2003.

Vonada, Damaine. *Ohio Matters of Fact,* 2nd ed. Wilmington, OH: Orange Frazer Press, 1990.

Wilkinson, Christina. *Bicentennial Barns of Ohio: A Tribute to the Barns and Their Owners*. Mentor, OH: Rosewood Press, 2003

www.dnr.state.oh.us/news/may04/0521/bigtree/tabid/12933/Default.aspx

www.dnr.state.oh.us/trees/buckeye_oh/tabid/5343/Default.aspx

http://en.wikipedia.org/wiki/Aesculus_glabra http://en.wikipedia.org/wiki/Aesculus_hippocastanum

http://en.wikipedia.org/wiki/William_Henry_Harrison

http://ohioline.osu.edu/b700/b700_02.html

www.oplin.org/tree/fact%20pages/buckeye_ohio/buckeye_ohio.html

http://plants.usda.gov/java/profile?symbol=AEGL

Two Worlds Collide

"Amish Buggy Safety in Ohio: Status Report and Recommendation, May 2000." Columbus: Ohio Department of Public Safety, 2000.

BIBLIOGRAPHY

"Amish Buggy Safety: When Horses Meet Horsepower,"
  Columbus: Ohio Department of Public Safety, July/August
  2008.

Baskin, John, and Michael O'Bryant, eds. *The Ohio Almanac: An
  Encyclopedia of Indispensable Information About the Buckeye
  Universe,* 3rd ed. Wilmington, OH: Orange Frazer Press, 2004.

Bender, Sue. *Plain and Simple: A Woman's Journey to the Amish.*
  San Francisco: Harper San Francisco, 1989.

Good, Merle and Phyllis. *20 Most Asked Questions About the Amish
  and Mennonites,* rev. ed. Intercourse, PA: Good Books, 1995.

Heinrichs, Ann. *America the Beautiful: Ohio.* New York and
  Danbury, CT: Children's Press, 1999.

Hope, James, and Susan Failor. *Bountiful Ohio: Good Food and
  Stories from Where the Heartland Begins.* Bowling Green, OH:
  Gabriel's Horn Publishing, 1993.

Hurwitz, Laura, photographs by Amanda Lumry and Loren
  Wengerd. *Holmespun: An Intimate Portrait of an Amish and
  Mennonite Community.* Bellevue, WA: Eaglemont Press, 2002.

Kraybill, Donald B. *The Riddle of Amish Culture,* rev. ed.
  Baltimore: Johns Hopkins University Press, 2001.

Rodgers, Ann. "Two Recent Crashes of Amish Buggies with Autos
  Raise Safety Issue." *Pittsburgh Post-Gazette,* May 25, 2008.

Rutti, Ron. "Amish boy dies, his 3 brothers hurt after van strikes
  their cart as they head for school." Cleveland.com, September
  18, 2008.

Schreiber, William I. *Our Amish Neighbors.* Chicago: University of
  Chicago Press, 1962.

"This Sign Means Caution: Driving Safely in Amish Country."
  Ohio State University Fact Sheet AEX-596-08, 2008.

www.ag.ohio-state.edu/~agsafety/ash/programs/am_smve.html

www.amish-heartland.com/amish/article/1940161

http://blog.cleveland.com/metro/2008/11/trumbull_county_man_
indicted_f.html

http://en.wikipedia.org/wiki/Amish

www.gameo.org/encyclopedia/contents/H6567.html

www.mapministry.org/news.php

www.ohiohistorycentral.org/entry.php?rec=573

http://pittsburgh.about.com/cs/pennsylvania/a/amish/htm

http://web.missouri.edu/~hartmanj/rs150/papers/2sudduthfs00
.html

Ohio Facts and Trivia

Baskin, John, and Michael O'Bryant, eds. *The Ohio Almanac: An Encyclopedia of Indispensable Information About the Buckeye Universe,* 3rd ed. Wilmington, OH: Orange Frazer Press, 2004.

Booth, Stephane Elise. *Buckeye Women: The History of Ohio's Daughters*. Athens: Ohio University Press, 2001.

Crawford, Brad, photography by William Manning. *Ohio: An Insider's Guide.* New York: Compass American Guides, 2005.

Flannery, Tim, and Peter Schouten. *A Gap in Nature: Discovering the World's Extinct Animals*. New York: Atlantic Monthly Press, 2001.

Goodman, Rebecca, and Barrett J. Brunsman. *This Day in Ohio History*. Cincinnati, OH: Emmis Books, 2005.

Hatcher, Harlan. *Buckeye Country: A Pageant of Ohio.* New York: H. C. Kinsey & Company, 1940.

Havighurst, Walter. *Ohio: A History.* Urbana and Chicago: University of Illinois Press, 2001.

Hope, James, and Susan Failor. *Bountiful Ohio: Good Food and Stories from Where the Heartland Begins*. Bowling Green, OH: Gabriel's Horn Publishing, 1993.

Knepper, George W. *Ohio and Its People*. Kent, OH: Kent State University Press, 2003.

The Land We Call Ohio: 88 Counties, 88 Paintings, 88 Histories. Project coordination and editing by John W. Hoberg, profiles by Deborah Bradford Linnville, paintings by Richard M. Canfield. Columbus, OH: Paint Ohio, LLC, 2003.

Martin, Michael A. *World Almanac Library of the States: Ohio*. New York: World Almanac Library, 2002.

Montgomery, Janine, and Kathy Akers. *Let's Discover Ohio. Student's Ed.* Kettering, OH: Schuerholz Graphics, 1995.

Noble, Allen G., and Albert Korsok. *Ohio: An American Heartland*. Columbus: Ohio Department of Natural Resources, 1975.

Ohio Atlas and Gazetteer. Freeport, ME: DeLorme Mapping Company, 1987.

Ohio Trivia, rev. ed. Compiled by Ernie and Jill Couch. Nashville, TN: Rutledge Hill Press, 1992.

Peacefull, Leonard. *A Geography of Ohio*. Kent, OH: Kent State University Press, 1996.

Perry, Dick; photography by Bruce Goldflies. *Ohio: A Personal Portrait of the 17th State*. Garden City, NY: Doubleday & Company, 1969.

Royster, Jacqueline Jones. *Profiles of Ohio Women 1803–2003*. Athens: Ohio University Press, 2003.

Schmidlin, Thomas W., and Jeanne Applehans Schmidlin. *Thunder in the Heartland: A Chronicle of Outstanding Weather Events in Ohio*. Kent, OH, and London: Kent State University Press, 1996.

Schonberg, Marcia, illustrated by Bruce Langton. *B is for Buckeye: An Ohio Alphabet.* Chelsea, MI: Sleeping Bear Press, 2000.

Stille, Sam Harden. *Ohio Builds a Nation: A Memorial to the Pioneers and the Celebrated Sons of "the Buckeye State,"* 4th ed. Lower Salem, OH, Chicago, and New York: The Arlendale Book House, 1953.

The Writers Program. *The Ohio Guide.* State of Ohio. Part of the Federal Writers Project, 1940.

Uncle John's Bathroom Reader Plunges into Ohio. San Diego and Ashland, OR: Bathroom Reader's Institute, 2007.

Vonada, Damaine. *Ohio Matters of Fact*, 2nd ed. Wilmington, OH: Orange Frazer Press,1990.

Willis, James A., Andrew Henderson, and Loren Coleman. *Weird Ohio: Your Travel Guide to Ohio's Local Legends and Best Kept Secrets.* New York: Sterling Publishing, 2005.

http://changingminds.org/disciplines/communication/color_effect.htm

http://en.wikipedia.org/wiki/List_of_festivals_in_Ohio

http://en.wikipedia.org/wiki/List_of_festivals_in_the_United_States

www.2.dot.state.oh.us/se/coveredbridges

http://infoplease.com/spot/colors1.html

www.festivalusa.com/states/ohiofest.htm

www.ohio.com/lifestyle/ohio_travel/8626922.html

www.runwalkjog.com/ohio_ffestivals.htm

www.usatoday.com/news/nation/2005-11-24-covered-bridges_x.htm

INDEX

ABOUT THE AUTHORS

Editor and author Carol Cartaino has been an Ohioan for more than thirty years, and in a lifetime of working on books has written and edited a wide range of nonfiction subject matter. She is the coauthor of *Keeping Work Simple* and *Get Organized, Get Published!* Carol lives and works in rural Seaman, Ohio, with her son, Clayton Collier-Cartaino, and more cats and other critters than she wishes to admit to.

Denvis O. Earls was born in Hamilton, Ohio. A professor of American history, Denvis is the author of *Church Belles: A Ministry for Confederate Christian Women, 1861–1865* and *Daughters of God: Southern Baptist Women in the Pulpit.* He lives in Wilmington, Ohio, with his wife, Linda, and a very energetic Jack Russell terrier named "Moochie."